MW01615760

Ramona
and Round About

Ramona and Round About

A history of San Diego County's little known back country

By
Charles R. LeMenager

To Nancy

Copyright © 1989 by Charles R. LeMenager

Second Printing 1990
Third Printing 1995

Printed in the United States of America

Library of Congress Catalogue Card Number 89-085175
International Standard Book Numbers:
Hardcover Edition: 0-9611102-1-X
Perfect Bound Edition: 0-9611102-2-8

Published by:

Eagle Peak Publishing Company
P.O. Box 1283
Ramona, California 92065

Cover design by Ernest Prinzhorn

Table of Contents

Prologue

It occurred to me there can't be too much difference between writing a history book and mining. Both take a heck of a lot of pick and shovel work.

But some diggings can be much more productive than others. That's when you're into real pay-dirt. Putting a chronicle together which covers such a wide range of subjects, was possible only because I was permitted to work several pretty rich veins. The experience was challenging and most educational.

While I did research as far away as the Bancroft Library in Berkeley, the State Library in Sacramento, the Arizona Historical Society in Tucson, and the Lahaina Restoration Foundation in Maui, the two most fruitful sources proved, naturally, to be right here in our own back yard.

The Ramona Pioneer Historical Society with the dedicated leadership of Guy Woodward, has amassed a great amount of Ramona area memorabilia. Guy's continual, but gentle persuasion with local pioneers for donations of heirlooms has resulted in a wide collection of historical information and artifacts. His full-time devotion to the development and preservation of the society's museum and archives will be appreciated for generations to come.

One resource in particular which the writer found to be extremely valuable is a collection of back copies of the Ramona Sentinel, which only recently were made available to the public. In 1983, the new owner of that newspaper, and his managing editor Thomas Fengler donated a vast library of issues going all the way back to 1914. These rare issues had been stored away and previously unavailable to the community.

Many hours of volunteer work subsequently went into combing thousands of issues for interesting items. The volunteer who spent by far the most time on that project was Jacqueline Beck. We were fortunate to be able to draw from the many volumes of typewritten summaries she prepared.

The San Diego Historical Society has a world-renowned library in Balboa Park. The major share of credit for that fine operation has to go to three devoted professionals. Sylvia Arden, head librarian who recently retired to an active life of consulting in this field, and Jane and Larry Booth who have managed the photo collection for many years. They, and their volunteers have always been most helpful to me in the years spent on research for this book and my first book, "Off the Main Road".

Hopefully the results of this effort will be received in the same spirit in which the author has approached the project. I attempted to cover a lot of territory and do it objectively. Even with the best of intentions, however, one is apt to miss some very important aspects. And undoubtedly there are probably a few errors.

But your comments and corrections are invited, and if there is a second printing, I will be most happy to set the record straight. In the meantime I hope you enjoy the book, and that maybe something I did or said here will inspire you and others to do some research and writing about our local heritage.

San Vicente Valley,   CRL
Ramona, California
August, 1989

1

Setting

The unincorporated township we know today as Ramona takes in about 75 square miles, that is if we go with boundaries set by the water district and regional planners.

But in attempting to chronicle a history of the area, we have to look beyond political boundaries and consider the influence the town represents as the center of San Diego County's back country. Historically, we should examine the settlements that were home to the area's early pioneers. Some of these settlements have given way to the development of Ramona and for the most part are no longer prominent today.

That's why this book is called **Ramona and Round About**. The 'Round About' part has a lot to do with Ramona's roots. Towns and hamlets ranging from Julian, Santa Ysabel, Ballena, Witch Creek and Mesa Grande to the north and east, and those in the south and west such as Foster, Woodson, Poway, San Pasqual and Highland Valley have played an important part in Ramona's heritage.

Newcomers walking the streets of Ramona today often

express surprise in finding little if any evidence of past affluence about the town. There are no splendid old mansions which were financed from gold mining or cotton money or were built by coal, timber or copper barons. The closest Ramona came to a show of early day wealth, is the Verlaque house on Main Street and the Amy Strong 'Castle' situated at the foot of Mount Woodson.

No, the bulk of Ramona's history is not found in affluence of the past, but in actions and events that involved its mainstream people - its early pioneers who were a part of that large human movement that started coming to California after the completion of the transcontinental railroad in 1869. These were settlers seeking a healthier climate and looking to improve their lot. They were the ones who put Ramona on the map.

Those of us who came in the later part of this century were, for the most part, seeking escape from urban pressure and looking for the peace and quiet expected from rural living.

Not a whole lot of cash money was ever generated from non-agricultural pursuits in Ramona until recent years. Even today, most of the 'new' money that flows into town, comes from paychecks earned by commuters working 'down the hill', from recreationites on their way to the mountains and desert, and from the growing number of senior citizens cashing retirement checks at local banks and markets. Neither has the town done well at creating many non-service related jobs. Maybe that's the way most Ramonans want to keep it. Quien sabe? (who knows?)

Aside from her people, Ramona has her own distinctive geographic personality. The beautiful semi-desert valleys and chaparral covered hills, ranging from gentle slopes to fierce granite bouldered mountains, give her a variety of landscape seldom found elsewhere. Not only is the visual result one of rare beauty, but the numerous surrounding ranges provide a welcome barrier against creeping air pollution spawned by the not too distant urban centers.

Profiles of mountains on the horizon have played a part in naming more than one local place. If we look southwest of town at the outline of the hills 4 to 5 miles distant, and if we squint our eyes and -- use a lot of imagination, it is possible to see what the Fanciscan Padre Mariner saw in 1779, the profile of a woman lying on her back, head on the left and feet to the right. It is said he named the valley for Saint Mary because of that silhouette.

About seven miles further east of Ramona, we can stand where the Old Julian Highway joins State Highway 78, and see in the hills to the north the outline of a giant whale, or 'ballena' in Spanish. The name Ballena, may well have been given the valley by one of the area's first white land owners, Captain Edward Stokes who had been an officer on whaling ships during the 1830s. Archives reveal no hint of that name being used in this area until after Stokes arrived in 1844.

During the 1860s and 70s, Ballena was one of San Diego County's most significant back country settlements, predating Nuevo (later renamed Ramona) by more than two decades. Today it houses far less people than it supported at the turn of the twentieth century - highly unusual in a County where practically every other pioneer hamlet has seemingly exploded with immigrants. Actually, more race horses today call Ballena home than do human beings. The most noticeable development is the Golden Eagle Ranch, where thoroughbred racehorses are bred and trained.

Further east is Witch Creek, Santa Ysabel and Mesa Grande, none of which were named after shapes on the horizon. Witch Creek's name came from superstitious Indians who feared evil spirits in the local creek. Santa Ysabel to the east, and San Vicente further south were named for patron Saints, as was the custom when large land grants were requested from the Mexican governors of early California.

One northern off-shoot of the Santa Maria grant is called Goose Valley, intersected today by Magnolia Ave and its extension, Black Canyon Road. Its name came about in the 1880s as a shortening for the name Valle de los Amigos, meaning in Spanish "Valley of Friends". The name was given it by a group of Friends Church members who settled there. Soon most of the locals found it easier to say goose than amigos. Before the Quakers, however, the valley was called Rincon Refugio, no doubt a name given it by the Stokes family. Adolfo Stokes built and lived in the home which still stands on Highway 78, just east of Magnolia. Adolfo's mother was Refugio Ortega Stokes.

Pamo Valley lies north of the main part of Santa Maria. The early Spanish missionaries referred to all of what we know today of Santa Maria and Pamo Valleys as Valle de Pamo. Pamo, pronounced 'pah-moo', is a Diegueno word meaning 'big horn sheep watering place'. Until recent times big horn sheep were still drinking in Coyote Canyon.

San Vicente Valley lies 5 miles southeast of Ramona towncenter. It was home to Augustus Barnett in the latter part of the 19th century. Today it is home to nearly 7,000 who reside in the master planned community of San Diego Country Estates, and accounts for over 25% of Ramona's population and nearly a third of its assessed valuation. In 1970 there were but four families living in the valley.

Today, (1989), a consensus of local authority places the current population within the Ramona planning area at between 25,000 and 27,000. Like most areas of San Diego County, the region has experienced extraordinary growth during the past two decades. From about 5,000 in 1970, Ramona has grown 500% in less than twenty years.

With few exceptions, little evidence remains today of

HILLS TO THE SOUTHWEST OF SANTA MARIA VALLEY. Mount Wood-son is on the right. It is said Father Mariner named the valley for the profile he perceived as Saint Mary shown between the two marks. Santa Maria's head is to the left and feet are to the right.

early day Nuevo (Ramona). The little town got its start in 1883 with the building of a general store and postoffice along a well worn wagon trail between San Diego and the booming mining town of Julian.

That first town building still stands, however, and continues to house retail business today. The first merchant's family build a home next door to the store in 1886 and that also still stands. Through the generosity of the Ransom family, the Verlaque house was donated to the community. With the leadership and hard work of Guy and Geneva Woodward, and generous contributions of money and countless hours of volunteer work from members of the Ramona Pioneer Historical Society, this old house and its grounds have been transformed into one of the country's finest small town historical museums.

While not many old Nuevo buildings still stand, there is one unmistakable imprint of early days that still remains and can't easily be altered. The main wagon trail to the mines became Main Street. Its diagonal slash across the valley, northeast and southwest forced the town's street grid to forever adjust, and its visitors and residents alike to continually wonder if one is traveling north or west - east or south when driving on Main Street.

2

First Inhabitants

When the white man recorded his first expeditions into the area in 1776-78, he found several Indian settlements. They were located in places ranging from the southern part of the Santa Maria Valley on the slopes of Mount Woodson, down into the northern reaches of Pamo Valley.

Today, signs of early Indian occupation can be found wherever there was once a reliable spring and oak trees from which acorns could be gathered. At one time these Indians roamed from the desert to the sea, and those who inhabited this area were known as 'Iipay. In more modern times they are referred to as Northern Dieguenos, the name given those who were under the influence of the San Diego Mission during the late 1700s and early 1800s.

Indian activities took place under the huge rock outcroppings on the Castle ranch on the flats of the old Etcheverry ranch, at the head ofClevenger Canyon, on the old Kunkler and White ranches, and near an old spring that flowed alongside Highway 78 near Santa Maria Creek.

Moving to the north end of the valley, archaeologists

have found remnants of a major settlement, or rancheria, located between Pamo Road and Lilac Street north of Washington Street. It is generally believed by anthropologists that the people who occupied this village hundreds of years ago, were some of the earliest settlers in the area. It was for these people that the name Valle de Pamo was given the valley before it was called the Santa Maria. The 'Iipay had strong ties between this land and the higher reaches of Black Canyon and Mesa Grande. During the summers they occupied the higher elevations, but when it became colder, made their home in the lower valleys. Another major village was located deeper in the Pamo Valley, at the confluence of the Santa Ysabel and Temescal Creeks at the 900 foot level. Further study indicates strong ties between these rancherias and those located further down into San Pasqual Valley.

The 'Iipay and Northern Dieguenos were bordered on the north by the Luiseno, Cupeno and Cahuilla, and on the south and east by the closely related Kumeyaay. Travel and trade were an important part of 'Iipay life. They established a network of trails which linked them with Pacific Ocean bands to the west and with the mountain and desert bands to the east.

The 'Iipay subsisted by hunting and gathering. They depended heavily upon the oak-pine resources found in their immediate seasonal environment, harvesting at the higher elevations in the summer and in the valleys during the winter. This practice often required outlying stations occupied by smaller groups from the parent villages, and these gathering and grinding stations have been found and identified in various spots throughout our region.

Deer, antelope, mountain sheep and small game such as rabbits, woodrats and quail were hunted locally. Seafood and desert plants were obtained by trade with other tribes. The people of Pamo also traveled to the ocean in the

TYPICAL INDIAN HUT USED BY 'IIPAY IN PAMO VALLEY. Young sycamores and slender live oak saplings were chosen for the posts of these huts. Holes were dug in the ground and the butts of the poles planted. Wild hemp or reed was used to lash the tops of these pliable limbs together to form a frame. Brush was used for siding and tied in rows, from the bottom up.

vicinity of Torrey Pines to obtain seafood on their own.

The men went naked. They wore a braided girdle of agave fiber which apparently was used for carrying, rather than for supporting a breechcloth. Footgear was worn only on rough ground and consisted of sandals made from agave fiber, cushioned to a thickness of half an inch or more. Both sexes wore their hair long, with the men bunching it on their crowns while the women allowed it to hang loose, but trimmed in the front at the eyebrows.

The Indians who inhabited the Valle de Pamo spoke the same dialect of the Yuman language as did the people of Santa Ysabel, Mesa Grande and Capitan Grande.

The first recorded contact between the white men and Indians of this area occurred in March, 1778 when it was reported the people of Pamo, one of the San Diego Mission rancherias, were getting ready to attack the Spanish. This was three years after the raid on that mission, which resulted in the killing of Father Jayme. José Francisco Ortega, commandant at the San Diego Presidio sent a warning to the Pamo rancheria. This message was met with contempt by their chief, Aaran. Ortega followed by sending eight leather jacketed soldiers under Sergeant Guillermo Carrillo, to enforce his warning. The Pamos had the help of four neighboring bands. But the Indians were surprised by the soldiers, who killed two and burned several who refused to come out of a hut. The rest were flogged while 80 bows, 1,500 arrows and a large number of

Bill Crocker Jr
64'

YOUNG BRAVES CAUGHT GAME BY THROWING CURVED STICKS.
Rabbits, woodrats and quail were stunned by boomerang-shaped sticks which were thrown along the ground to cripple the animals.

clubs were confiscated. The chiefs were convicted of having plotted to kill Christians and condemned to death by Ortega. There is no evidence, however, that the death penalty was ever carried out. Fathers Lasuen and Figuer petitioned the governor for a reprieve on their behalf and apparently the executions were cancelled when the chiefs started to show signs of respect for the church.

The nineteenth century saw the various small Indian settlements slowly but steadily squeezed out of the Santa Maria and Pamo Valleys. Those Pamos who physically survived the white man's dis eases, were either assimilated into his society as farm helpers, or driven further up into the hills and mountains. The U. S. Government in the late 1800s, established the Mesa Grande and Santa Ysabel Reservations on part of the lands the 'Iipay had traditionally used as their summer hunting and gathering grounds. This provided some of the descendants of the early Pamo inhabitants a final Indian "rancheria." It is believed other descendants also have become part of the Santa Ysabel and Volcan Reservations, and to some extent, the Barona Reservation as well.

Family names that evolved from earlier 'Iipay kin groups are still found locally today. Early kin names such as Letcapa "hard like a rock"; KwiLp or Kwitlp " name of a shrub"; and Kukuro "dark, shady"; have been retained and modified to LaChappa, Quilp and Couro.

The 1860 Federal census counted 202 Santa Ysabel Indians with Manual shown as Captain and Ventura as General. There were 125 natives residing at Mesa Grande, with Jose Panto listed as tribal chief.

In July 1870, Judge Benjamin Hayes camped at the former asistencia of Santa Ysabel. He noted that the old mission buildings were standing, but a new church had recently been built by the Indians and was being roofed while he was there. He visited the ruins of the church, the

CINON DURO MATAWEER, ONE OF THE LAST MESA GRANDE CHIEFS. (on left) and RAMONA PIÑA PREPARING ACORN MEAL. Photos taken about 1906 by Edward Davis at the Mesa Grande village of Tekemak.

MEN PLAYING PEON, POPULAR INDIAN GAME. The occasion was the annual St. Dominic's Fiesta about 1914. Setting was the village plaza formed by brush ramadas at Tekemak in Mesa Grande.

graveyard, and old zanja or irrigating ditch, and mentioned that the mission square was fully as large as that of San Luis Rey.

The 1880 census recorded 120 Indians living at Mesa Grande and 123 on the Santa Ysabel Reservation. In the twenty years from 1860, the native ranks living on or near the two reservations had shrunk by 20%. However, in the 41 years since Ortega had first sought the Santa Ysabel Grant in 1839, the population of that Mission tribe had drastically shrunk by some 80%.

In 1880 the census listed the Mesa Grande tribal captain as Duro Senone. Gaspara was recorded as Captain and Pablo as General.

The August 14, 1914 edition of the Ramona Sentinel

reported on the St. Dominic's Indian Fiesta held in the village of Tekemak at Mesa Grande. This annual event was put on by several Indian bands which occupied the broad area referred to by the paper as the Santa Ysabel Reservations. Included in the festivities were those from the Mesa Grande, Volcan and Santa Ysabel.

The setting was a plaza formed by the ramadas or brush houses of the Indians. "The plaza overlooks an arroyo chiquito on the west bank of which the Mission Church, rebuilt by Father Ubach in 1889 stands." So reported the Sentinel. The event lasted from Monday, ending early Friday morning, with mass held each day of the Fiesta by Fr. Lapointe, assisted by visiting padres.

"Horse racing, rooster pulling, wrestling and other athletic stunts, while peon games, klondike, dancing, imitation bull fighting and other amusements lasted long into the night."

After the fiesta, Hosea M. Osuna, policeman at Volcan announced that "after this year no more gambling like klondike, roulette or other American games would be permitted." The reservations' judge, Antonio LaChappa confirmed the directive.

Today, according to tribal chairperson Fern Southcott, there are over 400 enrolled in the Mesa Grande Band of Mission Indians. Of those tribal members, about 65 presently live in Mesa Grande. These figures have increased substantially since 1974 when there were 207 members on the rolls and 38 living on the reservation.

The Mesa Grande Band is comprised of descendants of a broad cross section of Northern Diegueno Indians. Many of them, however, are offspring of those natives who made their homes hundreds of years ago on the slopes of Mount Woodson and in the Santa Maria Creek plain; those who were really the first inhabitants of the area we now call Ramona.

3

The Administrator and the Captain

The first white owners of the area we know as Ramona, Santa Maria and Santa Ysabel Valleys were a partnership of two men who came from entirely different cultures and backgrounds. One was an elite Californian of Spanish heritage; the other, an Englishman who knew little of California until he sailed into Monterey Bay as captain of a merchant sailing ship. Why such a bond developed may seem unique today, but it was not uncommon in the California of the early 1800s. The Californio was José Joaquin Ortega and the Englishman Edward Stokes. They became related when Stokes married Ortega's daughter and later became known as Don Eduardo. Little to date has been compiled about these two that would give us an idea as to what kind of people they were, either as individuals, or how they faired as owners of over 35,000 acres of prime San Diego County grant lands. As it developed, the Californio would lose much of his share of the land due to bad debts, and the Englishman would not live long enough to enjoy his.

The Mexican governor of Alta California, Manuel Micheltorena in 1843 and 1844 granted them the Rancho Santa Ysabel and the Rancho Valle de Pamo, later renamed the Santa Maria. Each grant encompassed four square leagues or about 17,700 acres.

Records indicate that Narcisco Botello, a Mexican soldier of fortune, received a provisional grant to the Santa Maria soon after secularization of the missions. He apparently failed to meet the terms of the grant, losing his rights and leaving the land open for the later bid by Ortega.

Some claimed that Ortega used his influence and the knowledge gained as administrator of the San Diego Mission to carve out parts of the finest grazing and farm land from the old mission. While that may be true, there was more to the story than that. Many of the grantees during this period were officials or ex-officials in the Alto California Mexican Territorial regime, or related to them. During the period 1835, when the missions were secularized; until 1847 when the Anglo-Americans took control, Mexican governors doled out about 800 land grants. The last two governors, Micheltorena and Pio Pico alone, in the final four years of Mexican rule and in the face of sagging political fortunes, bestowed most of all the ranchos granted by that government.

Details of circumstances leading to the Ortega-Stokes relationship have long been lost, but we do know a few things of their backgrounds which provide some clues.

Don Joaquin

José Joaquin Ortega was baptized 1801 in Santa Barbara, one of fifteen children of José Maria Ortega and grandson of José Francisco Ortega.

Grandfather Francisco was a Spanish military officer who accompanied Father Junipero Serra and Captain Gaspar Portola, on their first expedition to Monterey in

1769. It is believed that while on this expedition, Francisco became the first white man to discover San Francisco Bay. Later he was in command of the guard at San Diego, where he witnessed, as expressed by historians, "the drenching of California pristine soil with the blood of her first martyr, Fray Luis Jayme." That was in November 1775 when the rebellious neophyte, Francisco "El Capitan de Cullamac" led the revolt against the mission. Sergeant José Francisco Ortega was a favorite of Junipero Serra, who in 1773 urged his appointment as commandant in California to succeed Pedro Fages. Serra's efforts failed, but he was made lieutenant and commanded at San Diego for eight years. In 1781 he helped found Santa Barbara, planning the buildings, fortifications and irrigation works and serving as commandant. He later commanded at Monterey as well, retiring as a brevet captain in 1795.

Joaquin's father, José Maria followed his father Francisco into the military, and eventually achieved the rank of sergeant. He retired early, however, in order to help pay off family debts. In recognition of outstanding service to the Spanish Crown, Francisco and son José Maria obtained the Rancho Nuestra Senora del Refugio about 1797. The name was later shortened to Rancho El Refugio and was one of less than twenty private ranchos granted under Spanish rule in California. It contained six square leagues and was located about 20 miles north of Santa Barbara, extending up the coast as far as Point Conception. The ranch was noted for its hospitality. El Refugio had its own embarcadero where ships landed to take on hides and tallow. Contrabandism was prevalent during the last decade of Spanish rule in California, and the Ortega's rancho was revealed as a haven for smuggling operations during the time of the Bouchard raids of 1818.

Don Joaquin was born and raised at El Refugio and came to San Diego sometime before 1821. That was the year he was married at the Mission San Diego de Alcala to Maria Casimira Pico. Maria was the sister of Pio Pico, the last Mexican governor, and Andres Pico, victorious leader of the Californios at San Pasqual.

After many years of pressure from Californios to get their hands on mission lands, and while sincere efforts were being advanced by leaders such as Governor José Figueroa for gradual secularization, the legislature in Mexico City abruptly decreed total secularization of the California mission system in August 1834. Neither the military officers at the presidios nor the civilians in the pueblos and ranchos could rival the power the padres had wielded for over 60 years. With this one sweeping decree, however, the mission churches were reduced to parish churches and their lands and assets taken over by the government. Such action was not unexpected, considering the anti-clericalism inherent in the Mexican revolution. The possibility that the Franciscans could continue to be allowed to hold some of the best land in California in the face of a growing, land-hungry population was highly unlikely. So it was decreed, no longer would the Franciscan fathers control the thousands of acres of rangelands, vineyards and farms they had helped develop.

Joaquin Ortega not only played a significant role as San Diego Mission administrator during the traumatic period that followed, but was a major player in the territorial politics leading to it. From 1834 to 1839, he was a member of the elite Alto California Diputacion, a seven member junta charged by Mexico City with legislative authority for the territory. Serving with Ortega on the junta that met in Monterey in 1834 were Pio Pico, José Antonio Estudillo, Francisco de Haro, J. A. Carrillo, C. A. Carrillo and José Castro with Governor Figueroa presiding. During this time, it should be noted, that in all the territory stretching along a 500 mile coastline from San Francisco Bay to San

Diego, the "gente de razon", or white population numbered less than 8,000 total. Major settlements were found near the presidios and missions. Monterey was usually the capital and other concentrations of whites were found in Los Angeles, Santa Barbara, San Jose and San Diego. Members of the diputacion were usually selected to represent these areas, and Joaquin, while spending increasingly more time in San Diego, represented Santa Barbara. An uncle, Francisco Ortega, had represented Santa Barbara in 1822 and had a hand in forming, and serving on the first Diputacion called under Mexican rule.

There is nothing in the published records of the 1834 junta meetings that indicate Joaquin took a lead in these meetings. He apparently was not one to make memorable speeches, or be overtly assertive with his peers. The make up of committees, however, probably indicates where his real interests lay. Like most political bodies, the Diputacion conducted much of its business in private. Joaquin served on such committees as Vacant Lands, Colonization and Industry and Agriculture. This could lead us to conclude that his active interest in land matters dated back long before his appointment as San Diego Mission administrator.

He was the first to hold that administrative position, being appointed by Governor Figueroa in April 1835. He was paid a rather handsome salary for the time - $50. per month - to come from mission income and proceeds from the farm products that the "emancipated" Indians were supposed to produce as before. The missionaries had managed the temporalities successfully without compensation for over half a century. As it developed, the hired managers, who lacked the type of leadership and managerial skills employed by the Franciscans, were able only to preside over the demise of the mission system.

Richard Henry Dana observed in 1836 that: "The priests

have now no power, except in their religious character, and the great possessions of the missions are given over to be preyed upon by harpies of civil power, who are sent there in the capacity of administradores, to settle up the concerns; and who usually end, in a few years, by making themselves fortunes, and leaving their stewardships worse than they found them."

Ortega was fired from his administrator's job in 1839 as part of a sweeping reform effort by Governor Juan Bautista Alvarado who was moved by the many Indian complaints about conditions at the missions. The Indians were "reduced to utter destitution," according to William E. P. Hartnell, the Governor's special investigator. He also reported that the Indians asked him to "remove the administrator and return them to the care of the Father, not because they had any complaint against Ortega, but because they realized that the Mission was not in a condition to maintain them." As part of this reform, the Pico brothers were also removed as administrators at Mission San Luis Rey. Ortega later served, however, as major domo of the Mission San Luis Rey from 1843-1845. While there he was believed to have taken considerable liberty with mission property, for as one former worker stated, he "appropriated to himself nearly all the mission cattle, but did not take any of its land. It was said that Sr. Ortega left the Mission stripped bare, making an end of everything, even to the plates and cups."

Judge Benjamin Hayes was to write in 1858, however: "Don Joaquin has been one of my steadfast friends, he was once administator of the Mission of San Diego, but never made money at this business, as many have done." Hayes also had kind words for Doña Ortega: "The wife of Don Joaquin is the sister of Don Pio Pico, of fairer complexion of any of the ladies of that family I have yet seen, kind and courteous beyond expression in her manners." The judge would learn, however, in 1863 during his campaign for re-election as district judge (a position he held with distinction for ten years), that friendships forged in politics can be easily bent and broken. Don Joaquin's nephew Pablo de la Garra was Hayes' opponent that year. While Hayes was considered the heavy favorite, he lost because he failed to carry the San Diego County vote, thanks mainly to Don Joaquin. The 62 year old Ortega wrote Pablo in Spanish, and in a shaky but neat hand: "Although your adversaries worked very hard, an old uncle with three friends accompanying him were more active than all put together." Ortega claimed to have campaigned in Pala, Portrero, Ballena, Santa Maria, San Pasqual, and all the way to the Colorado River.

Earlier, in the year 1851, Ortega was implicated in the famous Indian uprising led by Antonio Garra. In Garra's declaration before his military trial for murder, he claimed that Joaquin Ortega and José Antonio Estudillo had helped incite the revolt. These accusations, however, were denied and generally refuted by leading people of San Diego.

Don Joaquin appears to have been active in positions of influence most of his life. In addition to those mentioned previously, he was encargado de justicia of ranchos 1842-3, and justice of the peace in San Diego in 1843 and 1845. He was also active in the move to separate Southern California from the north in 1851. Ortega served on the committee which petitioned Congress to give them territorial status because of the inequitable way in which the State Legislature was taxing them. Eight years after California became a State, with San Diego as its first county, he served as a County supervisor for two one-year terms, 1858-1860.

Captain Stokes

While very little until now has been pulled together to paint a picture of Don Joaquin Ortega, practically nothing has been written about Edward Stokes. We do know, however, that during the 1830s Stokes was engaged as a first mate on whaling ships, and later into the early 1840s, as mate and master on various merchant ships sailing in the South Pacific and along the California coast.

Much of the merchant shipping activities along the California coast during these times involved the trading of cattle hides and tallow. San Diego was an active port in this commerce, having one of the best harbors for it. That apparently is how the Captain met Ortega and was introduced to his eldest daughter, 19-year-old Maria del Refugio de Jesus Ortega. The two were married at the San Diego Mission on June 12, 1840.

It was remarkable how many of the daughters of leading Californio families married Americans and Englishmen. According to historian Charles Shinn, writing in 1891: "The grace, beauty, and modesty of the women of the time were the admiration of every visitor. The freedom from care, the outdoor life and constant exercise, and the perfect climate of California had recreated the Adalusian type of loveliness. In the Ortega family, for instance, the women who all had brown hair and eyes, and were of pure Castillian stock; were so renowned for their beauty, that their fame extended to the City of Mexico, and General Ramirez came from there with letters of introduction to win a daughter of the Ortegas." The lady referred to by Shinn was none other than one of Joaquin's nine sisters, Maria de Jesus Salvatora Ortega Ramirez. The loveliness and charm of Ortega aside, Stokes was no doubt ready to settle down after more than 10 years at sea. Marrying into an influential California family, with real prospects of acquiring land must have held its attractions as well.

The earliest notes we find about Stokes come from a log he kept while first mate aboard the English whaling ship, the Sir Cockburn, which was being outfitted in late 1833 and sailed from Portsmouth for the South Pacific whaling grounds in February 1834.

The great era of whaling, which began in the 1820s and lasted until shortly after petroleum was discovered at Spindletop in 1859, was in its heyday. It was mainly whale oil that provided oil for the lamps of the world and lubrication for the machines of industry during that era. The Sir Cockburn was a full rigged ship, outfitted expressly for whaling activities. Whale ships were hunter, factory, warehouse and home for some 30 crewmen. The first three functions were usually handled with an adequate degree of efficiency. The forth left much to be desired. Life before the mast, in the forecastle where the ordinary seaman was quartered, ranged from barely tolerable to deplorable. Conditions for the mates weren't much better.

Stokes' log shows the Sir Cockburn, having left England on the 9th of February, didn't reach the Falklands until May 11th, and rounded Cape Horn May 27-30. June through August was spent hunting off the coast of Equador and Peru. While anchored at a small Peruvian port in August, Stokes noted the production of other whalers. The Winslow out of New Bedford, which had been seven months at sea, had 180 barrels of oil. The Pusey Hall, a fellow British ship had 100 barrels to show for four months toil. Stokes' ship had yet to kill and render a whale. It was three months later before they got their first two.

The typical whaler of that day produced about 2,000 barrels before returning to port or off-loading. A large sperm whale could yield up to 2,800 gallons of oil. But that was far from typical. The average yielded 25 to 30 barrels and

JANE COWGILL, A DIRECT STOKES /
ORTEGA DESCENDENT is shown holding Captain Stokes' original sea log,
over 150 years old, which he kept as
a first mate and master from 1833
until 1839.

CAPTAIN STOKES BECAME ACQUAINTED WITH THE ORTEGAS while
master of a merchant ship working the California coast in 1840.
Pictured on opposite page is a 1931 painting by Carl Oscar Borg. It
portrays a typical merchantman of that time trading with a Californio ranchero. Imported goods were sold from the ship much as a
general store. These were traded for cattle hides, carried to the shore
by ox cart and loaded in the ship's lighter by Indians.

it took 70 to 80 kills before a ship's quota could be made. A typical whaler's tour at sea lasted two to three years in those days, but the Sir Cockburn's voyage was obviously beginning to show all the ear-marks of a very long ordeal. Stokes' log gives no hint as to why things were not going well.

After working 15 months on the Sir Cockburn, and with only two whale kills to show for it, Stokes left her in Samoa and signed on the U.S. whaler, Merrymack out of Newbury. Five months later, in July 1835 he made another change to the whaler Amazon, and while aboard her, ran across the Sir Cockburn in September. His old shipmates reported having only 170 barrels of oil after hunting for 20 months.

Stokes left the oily decks of the "spouters" (whaling ships) in December 1835 to walk the white, holy-stoned decks of merchant ships for a while. He signed on in Hawaii as first mate on the Rasslas of Boston for "performance of a voyage" to Canton and Kamschatka. In October 1837, Stokes got his own command, as master of the merchant schooner Riatea. For the next three years he sailed mainly in Hawaiian waters, commanding both whalers and merchant ships.

Maritime records indicate that from 1840 to 1843, Stokes' activities were confined to merchant shipping along the California coast where he traded with many of the Californio rancheros.

During the 1830s and 40s, the California economy depended on production of cattle for hides and tallow. Some sheep were being grazed and the Californios grew grain and wine grapes. The merchant ships were floating trading posts, providing the means for commerce and trading imported goods for hides and tallow. Local products traded included not only the basic cattle bi-products and furs, but also increasing amounts of soap, vaquetas (tanned hides), aquardiente (hard liquor), saddles, boots and figs. Trade in aguardiente and wine proved to be a lucrative business, although it involved marketing problems which included stealing, evaporation in storage and leaking barrels.

After Stokes and his father in law received the grants to the Santa Maria and the Santa Ysabel, the sea capitain took up residence on dry land. Letters show that Stokes, while tending the Rancho Santa Maria, continued to do some trading. He sold San Diego merchant Captain Henry Fitch otter skins and wine in 1844 and 1845. But Stokes complained about his confinement on the ranch and referred to himself as a prisoner.

What little is found in published accounts about the gentleman named Edward Stokes, is virtually limited to notes made by Lt. W. H. Emory while he was with General Kearny's expedition in 1846. Even this account, unfortunately, gives Stokes but a cameo role, albeit a striking one to hear Emory relate it. Just prior to the fateful engagement with Andres Pico's lancers at San Pasqual, Kearny's men encamped near the Aqua Caliente Springs on the J. J. Warner rancho (Warner's Springs). The lieutenant described the scene as follows: "Above us was Mr. Warner's backwoods, American looking house, built with adobe and covered with thatched roof. Around were the thatched huts of the half naked Indians, who were held in a sort of serfdom by the master of the rancheria. I visited one or two of these huts, and found the inmates living in great poverty. The thermometer was at 30 degrees, they had no fires, and no coverings but sheepskins. They told me that when they were under the charge of the missions they were all comfortable and happy, but since the good priest had been removed, and the Missions placed in the hands of the people of the country, they had been ill-treated. This change took place in 1836, and many of the missions passed

THE ASISTENCIA OF SANTA YSABEL as it appeared in 1855 when this wood cut was made. It has been said that Edward Stokes had moved into the chapel and was living there at the time General Kearny's army reached Warner's springs in December 1846. Lt. W.H. Emory's journal spoke of Stokes living 15 miles distant from the springs, which if true, would put him very close to the asistencia. If Stokes wasn't living in the chapel, his residence in 1846 apparently wasn't far from it.

into the hands of men and their connexions (sic), who had effected the change." Emory continues: "Marshall (Warner's major domo) spoke of a Mr. Stokes, an Englishman, who lives 15 miles distant on the road to San Diego. The general at once dispatched Marshall to him, and in three hours he appeared at our camp, presenting a very singular and striking appearance. His dress was a black English hunting coat, a pair of black velvet trowsers, cut off at the knee, and open at the outside to the hip, beneath which were drawers of a spotless white; his leggings were of a black buckskin, and his heels armed with spurs six inches long. Above the whole bloomed the broad merry face of Mr. Stokes, the Englishman. He was very frank, proclaimed himself a neutral, but gave us all the information he possessed; which was that Commodore Stockton was in possession of San Diego, and that all the country between that place and Santa Barbara was in possession of the "country people." He confirmed all Marshall had said, and stated that he was going to San Diego the next morning. The general gave him a letter for that place."

In rendering aid to the Americans, Stokes demonstrated the kind of "neutrality" practiced by some rancho grantees during those confusing times. The very man who commanded the Mexican forces fighting Kearney, was no other than Captain Stokes' wife's uncle, Andres Pico.

Research has yet to conclusively determine when and where Stokes died. According to two accounts however, (testimony by J.J. Warner, and Juan Bandini at grant hearings) he died suddenly in Los Angeles shortly after the battle of San Pasqual, and before he was able to fully enjoy the fruits of his Mexican land grants.

A New Regime

Life for the old Californio Dons became much more difficult under the American's form of government. Like others of his class, Don Joaquin was land rich and money poor after the Mexicans lost power. Times were tough. There was little or no possibility for income from political patronage, and there was the ever increasing pressure of Yankee competition. Even his land rights were threatened if he did nothing about them. During their sunset years, Don Joaquin and Doña Maria Casimira resided on the Rancho Santa Margarita (now Camp Pendleton), and helped manage it for her brothers, Pio and Andrés Pico.

Don Joaquin's son Antonio and eldest brother, José Maria Martin lived on the Santa Maria as major domos and ran the two Ranchos for him and Refugio after Captain Stokes died. José Maria Martin was at Santa Maria when a party of the U.S. Boundary Commission rode through in 1849. Lt. Cave Couts who led the military escort protecting the party kept a diary. He tells of traveling to Santa Maria where "we find José Martin Ortega, a curiosity in himself. He is 68 years of age, and cares to talk of nothing but aguardiente (brandy) and women; is the oldest of 21 children, has had 21 himself". Several tax assessment statements made between 1851 and 1859 in behalf of Ortega/Stokes were signed by Antonio.

Refugio Stokes was remarried in June 1852 to widower Agustin Olvera, Los Angeles County judge, grantee of nearby Rancho Cuyamaca and probably best remembered as the man for whom the Los Angeles Olvera Street is named. Captain Stokes and Doña Refugio had three children, all boys. They were Alfredo, born 1840; Adolfo, born 1843 and Eduardo born 1846. Refugio and her new husband, Don Agustin, raised their new family, including the Stokes boys and Olvera's three daughters from his former marriage, at the Olvera home in Los Angeles.

While Captain Edward Stokes did not live long enough to fully realize the value of his land grants, his wife Refugio managed to preserve for their heirs those land rights that seemed so precious.

4

Land in a New State

For the first two decades of statehood, land titles and established rights to property throughout California were a chaotic mess. The situation in San Diego County's back country was no different. Those who owned land couldn't produce clear title in order to sell, and those newcomers seeking open land for homestead didn't know for sure what land was free because there were no official U.S. Government surveys.

Land conflicts which began in the early 19th century, came to a head in the 1850s, 60s and into the 70s. Involved were peoples from three different cultural backgrounds.

The native Indians were the first to occupy and utilize the land and its resources. They were intruded upon by the white man in the late 18th century, who came as Spaniard and missionary ostensibly to civilize and assist the natives in developing their resources. But with Mexico taking over from Spain and secularizing mission lands, the white man ultimately laid claim to much of the better farming and grazing land for himself.

With America's conquest in 1847, and discovery of gold in California in 1849 came the flood of land hungry immigrants from the more eastern parts of the continent.

Eventually it was the later group of people who won out, simply because there were more of them.

The Californio's Plight

The 1848 Treaty of Guadalupe Hidalgo between Mexico and the United States promised full protection of land rights granted by the Spanish and Mexican regimes. But the Gwin Act of 1851 which established a land commission, threw the entire burden of proof on the claimants. Grantees such as Ortega and the Stokes' heirs, were required to spend vast sums of money for Yankee lawyers and witnesses and for travel expenses to attend Commission hearings.

Until a patent was issued, grantees had no legal proof of ownership, nor title to convey. The U.S. Land Commission was but the first hurdle on the long road to a clear title under the new government. Most claims were denied, forcing the claimants into more legal expense in the appeal process.

In February 1852, Joaquin and daughter Doña Refugio Stokes were able to negotiate a sale for the Rancho Santa Ysabel to a Susan McKinstry. Susan was no doubt related to Dr. George McKinstry, Jr. who lived near the asistencia from about 1851 until 1859. (Their relationship thus far has escaped the author.) George was well known in Old Town, as the "far-famed doctor from Santa Ysabel". He held the distinction of being California's first sheriff, 1846-47, operating out of Sutter's Fort, and was known for having led the relief efforts for the famed Donner Party.

Records show total consideration for the rancho of $8,000. But more importantly, they received substantial up-front cash, $2,000 upon signing, and another $2,000 in

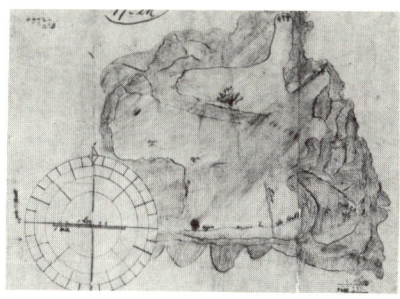

DESUENO (MAP) DRAWN BY CLAIMANT JOAQUIN ORTEGA was used as evidence in his claim for the Rancho Valle de Pamo, (Santa Maria). He presented this to the U.S. Land Commission in Los Angeles in 1852.

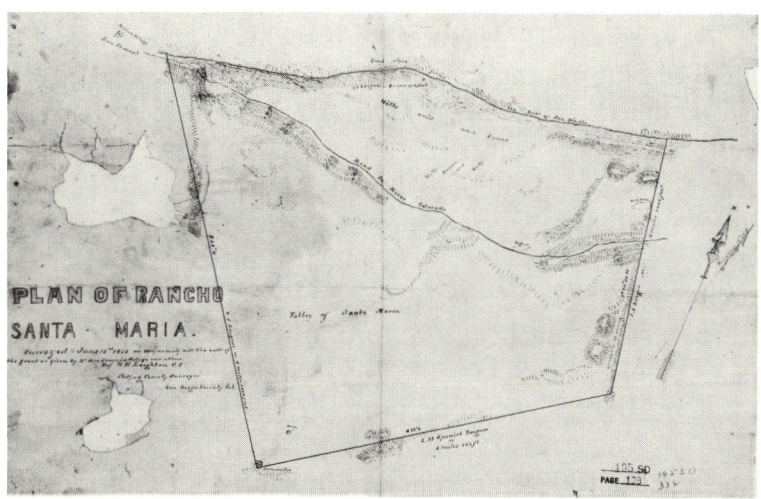

A SECOND MAP OF RANCHO SANTA MARIA, DRAWN BY A PROFES-SIONAL ENGINEER "in conformity with the calls of the grant as given by Don Jose Joaquin Ortega and others" in June 1856. Ortega's claim was denied by the Land Commission in 1852, as were most others. This meant the matter had to be settled in the Court of Appeals, where Ortega/Stokes finally received confirmation of the grant, but with adjustments. A Government survey in conformity with that court's decision, resulted in another major alteration to the boundaries in 1870. Compare these two maps with that final survey as outlined on page 64. This illustrates how chaotic land boundaries were in the first two decades of California statehood.

April 1852. The $4,000 balance was to be paid upon delivery of "a good and perfect title deed". Included in the purchase price were 200 head of cattle, 25 mares, one stallion, one bull and ten horses. The sale was never finalized. McKinstry paid property taxes on the entire 17,700 acres for the years 1854 and 1855, but by 1856, assessor's records show Ortega and Stokes as owners again. Apparently McKinstry became impatient with the time it was taking to perfect title and gave up on the deal.

The Land Commission hearings started in January 1852 and all sessions but one were held in San Francisco. A brief session was held in Los Angeles in the autumn of that year. Joaquin Ortega appeared at that session, petitioning for the Rancho Santa Maria and Rancho Santa Ysabel on behalf of himself and the Stokes' heirs. Witnesses included his brother-in-law Andres Pico, Able Sterns, Santiago Arguello and J.J. Warner.

Ortega was in need of even more cash in April 1852 and borrowed a large sum of money, for those days. Reasons stated were "for living expenses and taxes." He signed a bond for $1,587. to William C. Ferrell, mortgaging "all interest, right and title to one undivided moiety (half) of the Rancho Balle de Palmo (sic), better known by the name of Santa Maria." The bond bore interest at the rate of 8% PER MONTH, until paid. In agreeing to such a usurious rate (almost 100% per year), he must have felt confident in being able to pay it back quickly. Seven days later he did indeed reduce the principal by paying $446.87, plus accrued interest. But for the next 2 years, 3 months and 22 days, however, he made no further payments and Ferrell claimed Joaquin's half interest in the Santa Maria. During that short period of time, interest had increased the debt over three-fold to $3,669.68. It is interesting to note that Ferrell was also County tax collector at the time he was lending money to Don Joaquin and others. Ferrell also served as chairman of the San Diego County Board of Supervisors in 1853.

The two rancho grants were not finally confirmed by the Courts until 1859. Furthermore, the patents which were needed for conveyable title were not forthcoming until 1871, after U.S. Government surveys were certified.

The U.S. Land Commission processed 848 grant claims. The average length of time a California landowner had to wait for his patent was 17 years. (And we think Government is slow today!)

In the meantime, Don Joaquin filed in May 1854, under the California Act of 1852, for relief of insolvent debtors and protection from creditors. Like several other land rich, money poor Californio Dons, Joaquin's empire was slipping away.

In 1858, Refugio de Stokes found it necessary to file against her father and Ferrell for protection of the Stokes heirs' half interest in the Santa Maria. She petitioned the court for a referee to "fairly partition and determine a survey" of their land interest, which the court granted in December.

Don Joaquin died in 1865, having never realized full benefit of a clear U.S. title to the vast land holdings granted him 20 years earlier.

Records indicate the Santa Ysabel Rancho stayed in the Ortega/Stokes family until 1865-67 when a series of sales by brothers Adolfo and Eduardo Stokes finally disposed of all that ranch.

The American Settler

The American pioneers who were pouring into the new state in droves during the 1850s and 60s were looking for open land and new opportunities. They couldn't wait for commissions, courts, bureaucrats and surveyors. Many of

SAMUEL WARNOCK

JOSEPH SWYCAFFER

TWO OLD ARMY BUDDIES SHOWN IN LATER YEARS. Sam Warnock and Joe Swycaffer served at Fort Yuma on the Colorado River during the early 1850s. They were the first white, non Mexican grantee settlers in the general area we now call Ramona.

them sized up the situation and gambled that certain land upon which they settled, (or squatted) would soon be declared "Government Land", thus open for homestead.

Others simply became discouraged. Finding little good land left outside the vast Mexican land grants, many turned around and returned east.

Two of the earliest settlers, willing to take a gamble on future land rights were Sam Warnock and Joe Swycaffer. Recently discharged from the U. S. Army, they were among the first white American farmers to till the fields of this area.

They had served together as enlisted men at Fort Yuma, at the junction of the Colorado and Gila Rivers. The fort had been established to help protect defenseless emigrants and gold seekers from hostile Indians. While Fort Yuma was a benefit to the overland travellers, it was a 'hell hole' for those stationed there. Facing continuously hostile Indians, the soldiers were required to be ever on the alert. Poor rations, temperatures ranging from 112 to 132 degrees, and insects accounted for little sleep. The hardships at Fort Yuma took a heavy toll on the soldiers.

After their discharge from the Army, Warnock and Swycaffer made a living carrying Army mail between Fort Yuma, Arizona and San Diego from 1854 to 1856. They traversed a trail between the river and the coast that had been used for centuries by the Indians. It led through the desert to Vallecitos, where J. R. Lassator had built a "soddy" or adobe in 1854, up the east slope of the Cuyamaca Mountains to Green Valley and Cuyamaca Valley, then down to the San Diego River and Mission Valley. Each rode a mule and led a pack mule. The work was difficult and dangerous, taxing the endurance of even the strongest of men. The journey by mule from Yuma to San Diego was said to take the better part of a week.

The San Antonio and San Diego Mail Line was started

soon after in 1857, and used the same route as did the Army. Because they couldn't get wagons over that last mountain stretch, they used mules as did Warnock and Swycaffer, and it was that mail service which was dubbed "the Jack-Ass Mail".

The two veterans did some scouting around San Diego's back country. The Ballena Valley, with its springs and good grazing land, caught their eyes and they saw in it an ideal place to settle. Apparently, they calculated the valley would soon be declared public domain or government land, and thus open for later homesteading.

However, when Joaquin Ortega petitioned for the Santa Maria and Santa Ysabel he believed the two Ranchos abutted each other. In petitioning Mexican Governor Manuel Micheltorena in 1843 for the Santa Maria, which was supposed to contain four square leagues, he defined it as "bounded by Santa Isabel, the Pueblo of San Pasqual and the canon Santa Monica (El Cajon) and the canada de la Ballena including within said boundaries the watering place lately called Santa Teresa, having also for a boundary line the arroyo which is made by the River San Dieguito." Obviously, the amount of land contained within such a vast area described would contain more like 13 to 16 square leagues!

In later years it became apparent to many there was a large gap between the two rancho boundaries. Ortega either still believed that the boundary description concocted earlier would prevail even though the grants made it clear that he was entitled to no more than four square leagues in each rancho, or he didn't realize how much land mass was actually involved in his original sweeping description. In several dealings, in fact, he referred to "the watering place named Santa Teresa" as four square leagues of land which he owned. At the time he filed for protection as an insolvent debtor in 1854, he listed the Santa Teresa as an asset worth $16,000.

How Oretga could honestly believe he owned all that land between grants is hard to understand.

Warnock filed a preemption claim with San Diego County Recorder, W. Y. Couts on February 9, 1857 for 160 acres in the northern part of Ballena Valley. A preemption claim was a means, under Federal and State law, by which settlers could stake a claim to open land before it was officially declared eligible for homesteading. This was done by taking possession, recording a claim and making improvements. Once the land was confirmed to be open by official survey, the claimant would receive a homestead patent. This method of claiming land later became so abused throughout the State by fraudulent entries, however, that preemption laws were repealed in 1891.

Warnock sowed grain on the ranch in 1857 and was a major producer of barley in the county for many years after. The tax assessment statement for the year 1858 indicates Warnock was running 125 head of cattle and 60 head of wild horses.

Indian Land

Under Spain's Mission system, Indians were ultimately to be granted Pueblo status and enjoy the right of title to the California lands they helped develop under the Padres. The Santa Ysabel Indians farmed and grazed cattle under Franciscan supervision since the late 18th century. But in 1839, after Mexico took control of California and secularized Mission lands, Jose Joaquin Ortega petitioned the governor for a grant of that valley land. He claimed it was vacant and thus open to a loyal white countryman.

Padre Vincente Pasqual Olivas of San Diego Mission, however protested, "The locality of Santa Ysabel is not vacant land as the petitioner says in his representation; it is a Mission with a church, cemetery and other requisites of a civilized Pueblo, and a Priest does not reside in it only because of scarcity of priests. The Indians of said Mission have their plantings of wheat, barley, corn, beans peas and other plants for their sustenance, and two vineyards with their gardens, their horse stock; and in the summer their lands occupied with sheep. No private person can settle among a people of this class. And if the government would grant this land to the petitioner, to what point will it banish the Indians, now 580 souls?"

Five years later in 1844, however, only a relatively few Indians were still living there and the Mission's situation had deteriorated so badly that Fr. Olivas had to admit, "In consequence of there not being any possibility of improvement of the ranch of Santa Ysabel belonging to the Mission, all rights of the Mission thereto is ceded; there does not exist on said land more than a few crumbling walls and two vineyards." The land was thus granted to José Joaquin Ortega and his son in law, Captain Edward Stokes, but with the proviso that, "First, they will leave free the lands actually occupied by the natives of San Diego and moreover they will leave for the benefit of the Mission one hundred and fifty cows which Senor Ortega will give the community of Indians of the Mission." It was reported that Ortega killed 150 head in 1844, for the stated purpose of feeding the Indians, (no record is found of who benefited from the hides, however).

For the next few years, the Indians living near the old asistencia apparently fared well, according to one account. Cave Couts wrote, while accompanying the boundary commission on their way through Santa Ysabel to the Colorado River during the summer of 1849, "They have an abundance of chickens, eggs, melons, grapes, pears, etc. They are well dressed (some even dandily) and their Captain or General (Old Tomas Chihu) is our guide, and a great old rogue he is..." He further opined that the natives were far ahead of what he called common rancheros.

But the Indians' land rights at Santa Ysabel would remain in question another 25 years until the U. S. Government established reservations for them.

The Gwin Act of 1851, gave the U.S. Land Commission the duty of reporting to the Secretary of the Interior on the tenure by which the mission lands were held, and "those held by civilized Indians, and those who are engaged in agriculture or labor of any kind, and also those which are occupied and cultivated by Pueblos or Rancheros Indians."

Town officials worked to prove their pueblo titles while mission claimants did likewise. But because the Indians didn't understand what was going on, and did nothing themselves to initiate claims, nothing was being done to secure the land they occupied.

In 1856, after a bad year for Indian crops, and a shortage of wild edible plants such as acorns and mesquite, agitation for California reservations began to build. In spite of repeated pleas on the part of Indian agents through the Civil War years and into the reconstruction period nothing, however, was done by the U.S. Government about the land rights of the Mission Indians until 1870.

In an 1866 report to his superiors in the Interior Department, Indian Agent John Q. A. Stanley wrote, "the whites are pushing back on the frontier, and unless lands are reserved for the use of Indians, soon they will have no place to live." By 1869, Commissioner of Indian Affairs E.S. Parker and his superintendent for this area, John B. McIntosh had identified two large tracts of land in San Diego County which they felt were suitable and available, one in the Pala area and the other in the San Pasqual-Santa Maria area. It was estimated that a total appropriation of $28,160 would be necessary to establish the two reservations. This sum included $15,000 for cattle, food, farming implements, clothing and teams of animals.

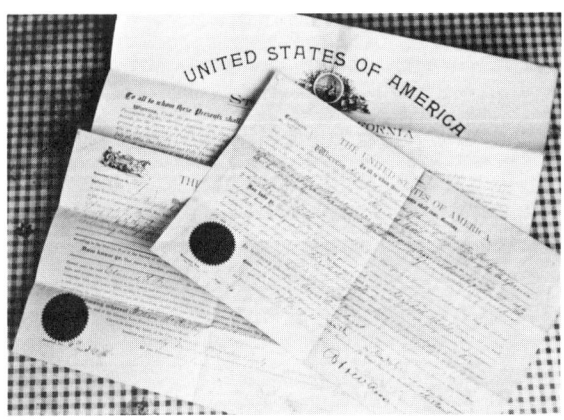

COVETED HOMESTEAD PATENTS issued to Mesa Grande settlers, signed by Presidents Grover Cleveland and William McKinley.

Finally, after years of pressure from local Indian agents, President U.S. Grant signed an executive order in January 1870 setting aside two reservations of land for Indians in San Diego County. One was the Pala reservation comprised of township 9 south, ranges 1 and 2 west, and the other was the Santa Maria-San Pasqual land which took in townships 12 and 13, range 1 west. Both reservations contained 46,000 acres each.

By looking at a map of the vicinity, it is clear to see that the latter took in the San Pasqual Valley and territory south, all the way to Mount Woodson, including Highland Valley and some of the western part of Rancho Santa Maria.

Needless to say, an immediate and loud cry was sounded by the white settlers affected by this action. Many of them had filed for preemption claims on land they had settled. The U.S. Government was still working on County land surveys, 20 years after California became a State. Until these surveys were finished and certified, no public domain land legally existed and these people had no right to gain a homestead title to the soil in which many had invested so much.

The settlers and land owners hired an attorney, who happened also to be a former part owner of the San Diego Union, and he was able to immediately bring the full force and power of the press to bear. Because of the settlers' strong opposition and of the Indians' natural reluctance to move onto these disputed lands due to strong settler reaction, President Grant revoked his executive order and returned the land in question to public domain in February 1871.

It took another five years before any reservations were finally established in San Diego County and until Congress eventually appropriated the money necessary to sustain them.

5

Transition Years

Until Gold was discovered in Julian, life in the county's isolated and spartan back country was uneventful.

Domingo Yorba's major domos, Ysidro and Librado Silvas were raising cattle for their absentee owner on the 13,316 acre San Vicente and Barona rancho.

Jesus Cheveria was major domo for Refugio Stokes Olvera at the Santa Maria Rancho, where according to County tax assessor's records for 1863, they were running 550 head of cattle on their 17,700 acres.

Sam Warnock, William Warnock, and Joe Swycaffer, having staked out farm land in the Ballena Valley, were busy growing barley and hay and raising cattle during the early 1860s.

The Civil War

The Civil War had little effect on San Diego County's back country, although the area was not totally untouched by that conflict.

Warnock sold grain to the Union Army stationed at

Camp Wright in Oak Grove, north of Warner's Springs. The Army considered Warnock to be a fair supplier, unlike some other area ranchers and speculators who had gained reputations as war-time profiteers. Major Edwin A. Rigg, commanding officer at Camp Wright, wrote Colonel James H. Carleton in Los Angeles October 25, 1861 concerning problems procuring forage. "I find that barley has been nearly all bought up by speculators, and 4 cents per pound is now asked for it. - but I found a man, Sam Warnock, who has 60,000 pounds of fine barley and will sell to the Government for 2 1/2 cents per pound. His barley is superior to what I have seen here."

Camp Wright was established on the Warner Ranch shortly after the outbreak of hostilities between the north and south. It was soon moved to Oak Grove where living conditions were much improved for the officers and men. The purpose of the Army's presence was to monitor travel along all trails out of southern California and intercept Confederate sympathizers attempting to return and aid the South.

Very little in the way of combat occurred in the area. However, as it developed, the only Civil War skirmish that took place in the whole State of California did happen in the Camp Wright sector. This involved the capture of the Showalter party at the Minter farm on Mesa Grande in December 1861.

Daniel Showalter was a prominent leader of the Southern faction in the California Assembly and represented Maricopa County. His reputation for being a hothead came to a climax when he challenged Charles Piercy, a Union supporter and assemblyman from San Bernadino, to a dual in May 1861. Differences revolved around the selection of General McDougall for the U.S. Senate, which broke the secession senatorial influence from California. The dual was staged in Marin County near San Rafael, because the judges in that County had a reputation for looking the other way at certain kinds of law breaking. Showalter shot and mortally wounded the 26 year old Piercy. As was expected, the victor got off scott free. Showalter's temper, however, was his ultimate undoing. His life also came to a violent end five years later in a bar in Mazatalan, Mexico, when he pulled a knife on an unappreciative bar owner after breaking up the establishment's furniture and fixtures. He was shot, his arm shattered, and died soon after from lockjaw.

Showalter had organized a party of 20 'Seceshs' (as secessionist sympathizers were called) in Los Angeles in November. Word got to Camp Wright, and the scouts were on the lookout. The party was tracked to a barn on the John Minter farm on Mesa Grande and a shoot-out ensued. No one was killed. But Showalter was captured and sat out the war in California, never to return to the Confederate country he had supported in the California legislature.

Post Civil War

By the end of the 1860s, Adolfo Stokes had married his half-sister, Dolores Concepcion Olvera, and moved from Los Angeles to the Santa Maria where he and his brothers built three adobe houses. (They were located north and east of the present intersection of Magnolia Avenue and Highway 78. The home which Adolfo built is still standing, and has been beautifully restored by its present owners. The other two no longer exist.) The brothers grazed cattle much as their father did 25 years earlier. Few others, but a hand full of squatters and Indians lived in the vast 17,700 acre valley. The rancho claim had finally been confirmed by the U.S. District Court in Los Angeles in 1858, and the patent was forthcoming in 1871.

Don Joaquin Ortega died in 1865 leaving his oft contested, and mortgaged half of the Santa Maria to his daughter Refugio and her three Stokes sons, Alfredo, Eduardo and Adolfo, who now owned the entire spread. In February 1870, the other three sold all their interest in the rancho to Adolfo for "$1,000 good and lawful money of the United States." For the first time since the Santa Maria became an entity, there was but one owner of the entire Rancho who finally held conveyable, uncontested title to the land.

With definition of Mexican land grant boundaries now final and U.S. Government surveys completed in 1870, preemption and homestead claims of settlers where being confirmed and patents issued throughout the area. Land was now being sold with clear U.S. title.

San Diego County started to experience a boom in land sales toward the end of the 1860's. This was due somewhat to Alonzo Horton's energetic promotional activities. The

ADOLFO STOKES WITH WIFE DOLORES OLVERA, SON ARISTIDES AND SIX DAUGHTERS. Pictured about 1887.

THE ADOLFO STOKES HOME AS IT APPEARS TODAY, 118 YEARS OLD.
The adobe has been beautifully restored with modern conveniences
and is located just east of Magnolia on Highway 78.

Rancho de la Nacion was bought by the Kimball Brothers
in 1868, who began developing the new town of National
City.

Apparently Domingo Yorba felt the San Vicente
Rancho was ripe for speculators and was ready to sell. A
group from San Francisco paid him "$8,000 in gold coin"
for his 13,316 acres in November 1869. This was before
completion of the grant land boundary survey.

It took less than three years after acquiring the rancho
for Adolfo to sell almost all the Santa Maria. In November
1872 he sold the ranch to Juan B. Arrambide for $40,000
in gold coin, reserving the 1,000 acre Goose Valley for
himself. By selling when he did, it appears Adolfo did
considerably better than Yorba had done with his San
Vicente sale. The $2.40 per acre he received vs Yorba's
return of $.60 was, on the face of it, four times better. Even
after comparing topography of the two grant lands, it is
apparent the market improved at least two to three fold
once a government patent was in hand.

Area's First Settlement

By 1871, the Ballena Valley had been developed into one of the finest agricultural sections in the County. During the dry season that year, 7,200 bushels of barley were harvested. Of this total Sam and William Warnock raised 2,000 bushels each and Joe Swycaffer about 1,000. The balance of valley production was raised by farmers whose means didn't allow extensive farming. Rye was grown as an experiment and proved a success with 12,000 pounds produced.

But hay was the biggest crop. Not because grain didn't do well there, but because the heavy travel to the mines in Julian created a tremendous demand for hay and it proved more profitable. It was estimated that during that year, about two thirds of all stock in San Diego County were being fed as a result of Ballena farmers' productivity.

The earliest official San Diego County base map was drafted in 1871, shortly after the official U.S. Government survey was certified. It shows all the rancho boundaries as well as township and range lines, (but no section lines). Shown also are all homestead and preemption claim lands in Ballena, San Pasqual, Poway, and other parts of the county.

Pioneer families settling in and around Ballena after 1856, when Sam Warnock first broke sod, into the early 70s, when the first official map appeared, include many claimants whose names are still locally familiar a century and a quarter later. Settlers during this era included such families as Littlepage, Bradley, Billingsley, Dye, McIntire, Casner, Brawner and McIntosh, in addition to Swycaffer and the Warnocks.

William Warnock sailed around the Horn in 1857 to join his brother Sam. The family located on the banks of Wash Hollow living in a ramada close to the Indians who had a rancheria there. This was temporary until Bill decided that

Santa Teresa Valley should be open for homestead and decided to settle there. This in spite of Joaquin Ortega's claim that the Santa Teresa was part of his Santa Maria grant. The matter wasn't settled until the U.S. Court of Appeals confirmed the grant as containing no more than four square leagues, and government survey determined Santa Teresa to be public domain. The oldest known home standing in the Ramona area today is the ranch house Bill Warnock started in 1859 in Santa Teresa.

Littlepage Road runs south from where Route 78 meets the Old Julian Road and leads to this pioneer family's homestead on the northern foot of Mount Gower. The Littlepages were among the earliest post-Civil War families to arrive in the area. They came overland with two other Texas families, the Martin Casners and Cal Putnams. The Casners settled west of Ballena and the Putnams in Wynola Valley near Julian.

By July 1870, the increase in Ballena population, as well as the traffic through the valley generated by the Julian mines, prompted Sam Warnock to open a store and post office. It was located near a spring where today stands the main gate to the Golden Eagle Ranch. The Ballena postoffice closed in 1902 and the people in the area used the Witch Creek office, which had been established in 1893, until that finally closed in 1936.

Captain Stokes was not the only sailor to leave his stamp on this area. An early pioneer who settled on land west of Ballena, but east of the Santa Maria grant was Danial McIntosh, Sr. He was a native of Nova Scotia and first mate who sailed merchant ships around the world. After over 14 years at sea, McIntosh retired to Scammon's Lagoon in Baja California but stayed only 2 years before moving north. He and his bride of one year, Romana, settled on their homestead in 1872 near the Santa Maria Creek (now called Hatfield), planting grain, fruit trees and raising

BALLENA TODAY IS HOME TO MORE HORSES THAN PEOPLE. From the 1860s to well into the 1890s, however, it was the largest settlement in the Ramona area.

stock. It wasn't long before the McIntoshs established a stage station at their house to serve travellers coming up the Barona-San Vicente trail, as well as those using the Poway route. They had six children, one of whom, Daniel Jr. was active in the community most all his life farming and hauling freight up and down the mountains of the back country.

Several of Daniel Jr.'s descendants are still living in the Ramona area. Among them are Louise Shidner, musician and artist (who kindly allowed us to use some of her paintings in this book), and former Ramona postmaster, Don McIntosh. Others who are active in Ramona include Linda McIntosh Thomsen and husband Art, fine examples of that pioneer heritage.

6

Roads and Transportation

One of the first written accounts of conditions encountered in trying to bring wagons up into the Santa Maria Valley was described by Cave Couts in 1849. The U.S. Boundary Commission was established shortly after the American conquest of California. Its survey party had set out from San Diego for the Colorado River with Lt. Couts, and his Company A of the First Dragoons providing protection for the party.

"From Santa Monica (El Cajon today) to this place, Santa Maria, about 14 miles," wrote Couts, "the road is very bad for wagons, and we have been four days of hard work getting through." Couts gives no details as to the route they took, but it was most likely an old Indian trail used by the padres that meadered up through Sycamore Canyon east of the present Poway.

Dr. George McKinstry later travelled regularly between his home in Santa Ysabel and Mesa Grande to Old Town San Diego on horse back during the 1850s. His diaries give us an idea of how much time it took for the trip. Leaving

Old Town late on the 5th of September 1859, he spent the night at Los Penasquitos. He wrote, "9/6, left at daylight, stopped at San Pasqual, breakfast at Pancho's, left by 10am, arrived at Mesa (Grande) 4pm."

The route he took generally followed the Indian trails up from San Pasqual through Pamo Valley and on to Mesa Grande. However, on other occasions, he refers to also using the "St. Vicente trail", through the San Vicente and Barona Valleys.

The following gives us an idea of what these pioneers went through to vote:

"9/7, went to Santa Ysabel 9am. Voted the Republican ticket. Pleasant day, cold night." Then nine days later, he wrote "9/16, Judge Hayes in at night, Election news Warner's District."

During the first 20 or so years that California was a state, every elector from Santa Maria to Warners Springs voted at the one polling place, Santa Ysabel. If the pioneer wanted to vote, and most of them did, they got on their horse and rode 'a pretty far piece' to do it.

With the discovery of gold in Julian on Washington's birthday 1870, back country travel required more than just horse trails. Roads that could be traversed by heavy wagon and stage coach were sorely needed.

Chester Gunn used the "St. Vicente trail" for his pony express mail service which he ran to the mines from the docks in San Diego. It came up out of the San Vicente Valley, joining the road to Ballena at Casner's place, not far from where Vista Ramona Road and the Old Julian Highway meet today.

This route became O.S.12, when the County board of supervisors declared it a "public highway" in 1870. But it was nothing more than a trail. Coming through the El Cajon pass, it crossed the San Diego River near Lakeside, heading toward Foster's (where the San Vicente Dam is today) then turned east up the mountainside, heading into the Barona Valley. This road was barely passable for lighter teams pulling hacks, once it reached the rocky hills and mountains. The heavier wagons had to take a different route in those early days.

Stages and freight wagons coming from San Diego used what was referred to by some pioneers as the Government Highway. It started by way of the Mission Valley Grade, up Murray Canyon, across the mesa near Camp Kearny, down a canyon into Poway Valley (spelled Paguay then), then north generally following the route we call Pomerado Road today, out the north end to Bernardo and up into Highland Valley, overlooking San Pasqual Valley, then across Santa Maria Valley to the McIntosh ranch and on to Ballena, Witch Creek and Santa Ysabel. This route turned north to Warners, Oak Grove, Temecula and eventually San Bernardino. However those going to Julian continued east up the mountain. This was a long way to Julian, some 60 miles, and the teamsters needed something more direct.

Some of the pre-Civil War Ballena settlers, such as Bill Warnock, would take this route north to San Bernardino to stock up on supplies. Old Town San Diego was hard to get to with wagon, and besides, it had little to offer. Warnock would make an annual trek north for such staples as flour, beans (if he hadn't raised enough that year), matches, denim cloth and the like. It was an arduous trip that was not only hazardous, but time consuming.

The mail and passenger stages serving the mines during the early 70s used this route south to San Diego for several years. The first stage service to Julian was started by William Tweed in 1871. Coaches left San Diego on Mondays and Thursdays at 6 a.m. and returned on Tuesdays and Fridays. Stewart and Reed's office on 6th near J Street, or Tweeds house on E Street near 1st served as coach stations. The fare to Julian was $6, but the return trip was $4.

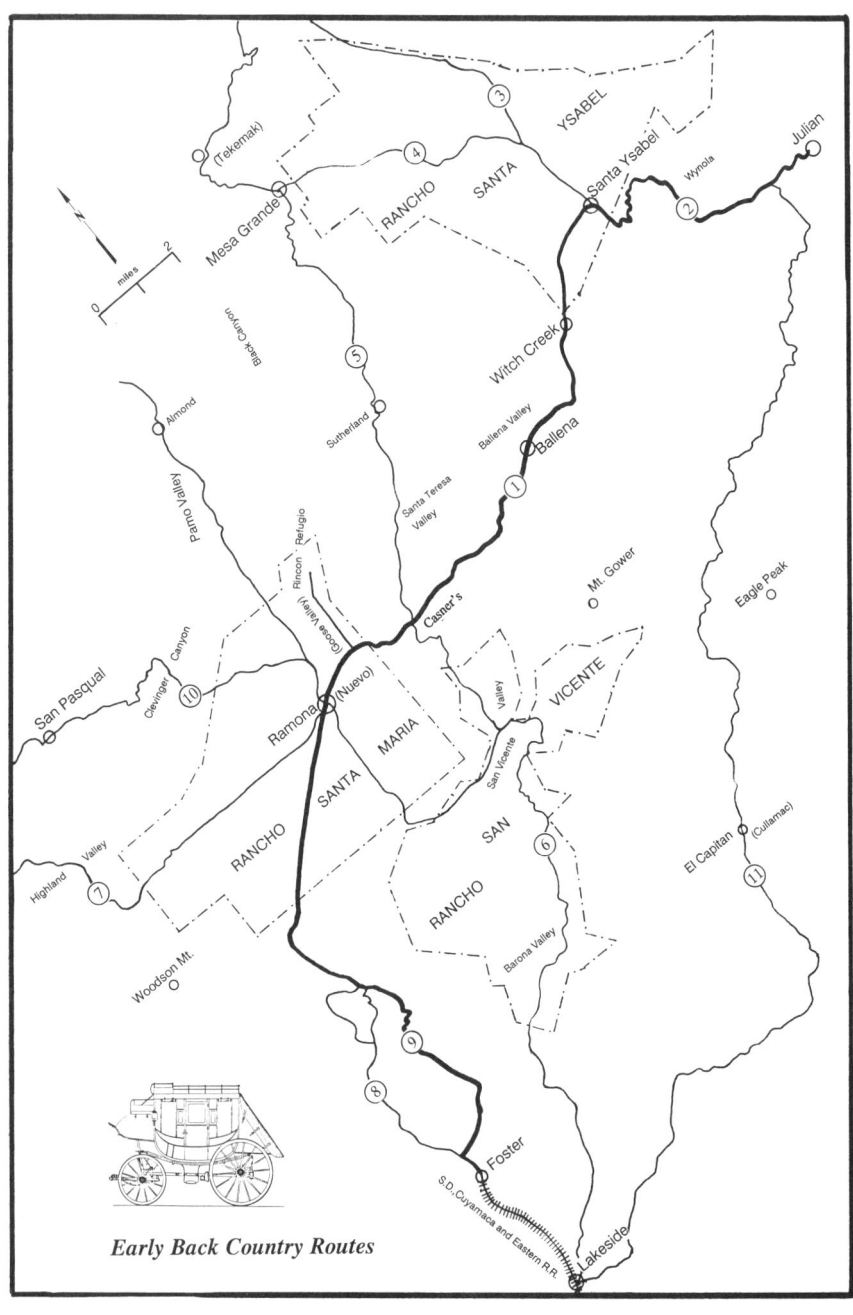

Early Back Country Routes

James Jasper wrote in 1928 about the fierce competition that developed between stage operators in the early 70s. "Seems that Adolph Stokes, who owned the Santa Maria Rancho, was well stocked with horses. Seeing an opportunity for some profitable employment he decided to go into competition with the Tweed Stage line, and a spirited rivalry followed. Fares were cut and re-cut," wrote Jasper, "foreshadowing the survival of the fittest, until passengers could ride the 60 miles between San Diego and Julian free. Then the opposition line offered one dollar to each passenger that rode with their driver. That seemed the limit, but it was not, for the next day the old line offered passengers one dollar each and free drinks on the way. The free drinks won and the opposition went out of business."

KEY TO MAP: EARLY BACK COUNTRY ROUTES

1. Main Road Santa Ysabel - Santa Maria 1840s-1930s, rerouted between Ballena & Santa Maria, through Santa Theresa, 1930s
2. Main Road Santa Ysabel - Julian 1870s - Today
3. Main Road Santa Ysabel - Warners, Oak Grove & Temecula 1840s-Today
4. Main Road Santa Ysabel - Mesa Grande 1850s-Today
5. Casner's - Mesa Grande 1870-1950 (Blocked when Sutherland Dam finished)
6. Casner's - Lakeside via San Vicente and Barona, Light Wagon and Ponies, 1850s-1900
7. Santa Maria - San Diego, via Highland Valley & Poway, Early 1870s, Freight & Stages
8. Santa Maria - San Diego, via Atkinson Toll Road, 1873-1888 (route altered to west 1875), Freight & Stages
9. Santa Maria - San Diego, via Mussey Grade 1888-1943 (Blocked when San Vicente dam finished), Freight & Stages
10. Santa Maria - San Pasqual, via Clevenger Canyon, Light rigs 1860s-1900
11. Julian - Lakeside, Eagle Peak Road, 1870s-1933 (when El Capitan dam finished)

The San Diego Daily World printed an account on July 28, 1872 of how fierce that competition really got between Stokes and Tweed:

Exciting Race Between The Pioneer and Mail Stage from Julian—Two Horses Ruined

From Col. Hopkins, of Julian City, and others we learn the following: At 6:20 A.M. of yesterday, "George" cried "all aboard" and almost instanter six passengers were rapidly whirled out of Julian, in one of Tweed's pioneer stages, drawn by four swift horses. Before reaching Rock Springs, the rumbling of Stokes' mail stage was heard, and a look back revealed, amid clouds of dust, the dim outline of four horses on the full run. Soon the "mail Stage," with two or three passengers, and Stokes himself for driver, came thundering alongside of the "Pioneer" and made a splendid effort to "pass." All was now excitement, drivers, horses and passengers, all anxious to run, except the Col. who is religiously opposed to racing. The wheels whizzed, the horses' feet clattered, drivers cracked their whips and lashed their panting, foaming coursers, clouds of dust filled the air and the excited passengers joined in the general din and "made the confusion worst confounded." Now the Pioneer would shoot ahead, and anon the Mail would lap and make a desperate but vain effort to lead George. This exciting and hazardous racing was kept up till near Rock Springs, when one of Stokes' horses stepped in a squirrel hole and broke his leg. The animal was quickly stripped of his harness, and on the Mail went, drawn by three horses. While the Pioneer was hastily dining and changing horse, Stokes got ahead. Soon one of his overheated horses "gave out" and, falling down, was stripped and rolled into a gulch. At Babb's, Stokes got fresh horses, and driving furiously kept the lead, and arrived in the city several miles in advance of the Pioneer. George, supposing that the Mail had taken the usual "Mail" route via Old Town, and some miles out of the way, and supposing also that the Pioneer was ahead, came in more leisurely - and behind.

Racing is always interesting because exciting, yet, we hope, bothe lines have shown their "metal" and "bottom," will, for the sake of the traveling public and poor horses, go at a moderate pace, except when the World is aboard."

Rock Springs was located just north of the present intersection of Poway and Pomerado Roads, and Babb's later became known as Big Springs Lodge and Poway Grove.

In 1873, two enterprising brothers, Lemuel and Henry Atkinson saw an opportunity to cash in on the bad road conditions. They were from Sacramento where their family had arrived from Virginia to mine for gold in 1852. When gold was later discovered in Julian, they moved south and went to work at the Golden Chariot where Lemuel was mine foreman. Realizing the need for a shorter haul to the mines, they studied the various possible routes, and filed on land at the north end of what is now Mussey Grade Road. In 1873 they built the Atkinson toll road on the opposite side of the mountain from where the Mussey is presently aligned.

After a year, however, they apparently figured more money could be made by selling the road to the county than by operating and maintaining it, and did so for the handsome sum of $1,700. Henry Atkinson was appointed roadmaster for that district by the board of supervisors.

In the meantime, Lemuel opened the Halfway House as a stage stop. In more recent times it has been referred to as the Atkinson Brother's Toll House. "It turned out to be a very successful business.", according to Frances Atkinson Moore, daughter of Lemuel, who recalled in 1979, "The

TYPICAL SIX HORSE TEAM FREIGHT WAGON hauling hay in the back country. Illustrated here is Dan McIntosh, general freight hauler around the turn of the century. IcIntosh could provide a 20 horse team if that's what it took to get a load up the grade. His teams were regarded by many as the best in the back country. Painting by Louise Shidner, Dan's daughter.

Chinese cook was a good one and as neighbors were few and far between, the Halfway House served as a meeting place to settle the ills of the word. Many were the arguments about politics and religion - the main topics of the day. If meat was scarce, all father had to do was throw a little grain out into the yard, get the gun, shut his eyes and pull the trigger, and there was a delicious quail dinner."

The Atkinson Road proved a real tough one to maintain. It was very steep in places, and when the heavy rains came, it was a nightmare for teamsters to negotiate. On April 25, 1883, the San Diego Union reported, "the road from the head of Atkinson grade to the Cajon is a disgrace to the County - it could hardly be in worse condition." Three weeks later Joseph Foster was appointed overseer for that road district. In spite of working long hard hours, however, Foster couldn't keep up with it. The paper reported on

THE CONCORD STAGE WAS THE PRINCIPAL 'PEOPLE MOVER' IN THE BACK COUNTRY FOR OVER 25 YEARS. The railroad ran only as far as Foster. From there up to Ramona, Ballena, Warner's Springs and Julian it was a bumpy, dusty ride on narrow, rocky roads.

September 25, 1883 that, "Joe Foster has been hard at work the last 10 days covering the grade with straw, but the road is in wretched condition."

The back country settlers had become impatient with the situation and in October that year, Bernard Etcheverry presented the board of supervisors with a petition to build a new road to replace the Atkinson. A survey had deter mined that a new route through Mussey's Cañon would result in an average road grade of 9 inches to the rod (4.5 percent), while the Atkinson grade ran in many spots, 30"-33" to the rod, (15 to 17 percent).

But the county was short of road funds (times haven't changed) and the supervisors determined that those people who would benefit from the new road should pay half the costs. A private subscription was circulated in Santa Maria, Ballena, Julian and vicinity to help finance

BY THE EARLY 1930s, MUSSEY GRADE WAS STILL PROVIDING A CHALLENGE TO TRUCKS AS WELL AS AUTOMOBILES. Here a rock slide is being cleared to open the road to backed-up traffic. As usual, John Barger (far right) was in the forefront when a big job needed to be done.

construction. It was thought that $1,000 in private funds could be raised and that sum would cover the county shortage. The $1,000 was raised with Etcheverry heading the list for $300. In May 1884, bids were received. Low bid was $5,200 from Geo. Lyons of Old Town. The board rejected all bids. Late rains had so damaged most of the roads throughout the County that there wasn't enough left in the road fund to even start work on the Mussey-Matthew Cañon Road (the name it went by at the time).

It wasn't until the following February that the project was advertised for bids again, and then only a portion of the total route. Money was not available to complete the project until much later, when a final construction contract was awarded in December 1886.

Mussey Grade Road provided the main link between Ramona and San Diego for over 50 years. From the late

1880s until the mid-20s, it remained a narrow, rocky, rutted, dusty road. After 1926, rubber tired motor vehicles enjoyed an all-weather two lane concrete surface. The construction of the San Vicente dam blocked its right of way, and the road was replaced in 1943 by a new north-south route, State Highway 67.

While the Mussey Grade proved to be the main route between the back country and San Diego, it wasn't the shortest way to go to Julian. One could save five miles travel to Julian, if he wasn't interested in going through Nuevo (Ramona) and Ballena, by taking the Eagle Peak Road. This road ran up the east side of the San Diego river basin through the Capitan Grande reservation and was used from the 1880s until El Capitan dam was completed in 1933. The City of San Diego, who built the dam, agreed to realign and replace the portion of road submersed by the reservoir but, according to Ed Fletcher who wrote in his 1952 memoirs, they reneged thus denying the mountain community their alternate route to the city.

7

One Room Schoolhouse

In the early horse-and-buggy days, wherever seven or more children of five years of age and older lived within walking distance, a grammar school could be established under the County Rural School System. School facilities for eight grades were built and certified teachers employed by the local taxpayers.

Ballena was populated with about 10 families by 1871, and as a result became one of the first rural school districts to be established in the county. Its district boundaries ran as far south as El Cajon, west to Poway, taking in the Santa Maria Valley, and east to Julian which had established a district a year earlier. Julian's boundary ran all the way east to the Colorado River.

Within those vast boundaries, Ballena had only 34 children registered between the ages of five and 15 years of age in 1871, while the Julian district had 65, Poway 60 and Cajon 21 students that same year.

With more people moving into the area, the Santa Maria School District was formed in 1881 and Ramona's first schoolhouse built, just east of the present townsite of

Ramona. It was built near a rock pile on the south side of the Julian Highway near Magnolia on land donated by a Mr. Budelier.

Some might rightly contend that the 1871 school house built in Ballena was actually "Ramona's" first school, since the present day boundaries of the Ramona Unified School District cover the site of that original school.

Teaching conditions in those early one-room school houses were far from idyllic, and apparently less so in Ballena than Santa Maria. Pay for the Ballena teacher in 1881 was set at $75 per month, while the Santa Maria teacher received $58.48. Ballena apparently had a much harder time keeping teachers - and for obvious reasons.

In 1934, Maud Thayer Frary told of how it was to teach in a 12 year old classroom in Ballena in 1883. "The school was tiny, about 12 by 16 feet, and I had 37 children there from four years old to 18. It was a pretty old school even then. It was built from Julian lumber and it warped, you could put your arm through a good many places. There was no ceiling and just the rough boards. My desk was a carpenter's bench, and I had a stool to sit on. The benches for the children were not screwed down. They sometimes got knocked over and all the books, ink, paper and every thing would be spilled on the floor." Getting drinking water for classroom use apparently was another challenge. "I had to send two children at a time over to Swycaffer's for water and they would get back with only about half a pail — not enough to go around." She went on to give more examples of why Ballena had a hard time keeping teachers. "The school house was in such a disreputable condition that the superintendent would not let me continue. The winter before, it had rained in and I could not get my clothes dried out all day. The superintendent said,'You will end like the other teacher.' One or more of them had gone into a decline (Butler had T.B. and Hamilton had it) and I caught one cold after another."

GENERAL STATISTICS.

1. What is the grade of your school? — *Primary*
2. How many pupils in High School Class?
3. How many pupils in Grammar Grade?
4. How many pupils in Primary Grade? — *Twenty One*
5. How many months have you taught in this School? — *Eight*
6. Number of school months school has been maintained during present year? — *Eight*
7. Monthly Salary of teacher? — *$55.48*
8. What journals of education have you taken?
9. Did you attend your County Institute? — *Yes.*
10. Were you allowed pay for time in attendance? — *Yes.*
11. Grade and date of your certificate, — *Life Diploma, April 1881.*
12. Number of school visits made by School Trustees, and average time spent at each visit, — *Six — Half hour*
13. Number of school visits made by County Superintendent, and average time spent at each visit, — *One — One and a half hour*
14. Number of school visits made by other persons, — *Thirteen*
15. Number of volumes in School Library, — *Ten (10)*
16. Have you kept the State School Registers as required by law? — *Yes*
17. Have you used in school the authorized Series of Text Books? — *Yes*
18. Have you followed the course of studies prescribed by the Board of Education? — *Yes*
19. Have you complied with the provisions of Section 1673 of the Political Code? — *Yes*
20. Have you suitable accommodations in your school house for all pupils who wish to attend? — *Yes*
21. Is your school supplied with suitable furniture? — *It answers the purpose*
22. Has your school sufficient grounds? — *Yes*
23. Are the grounds suitably improved? — *No.*
24. Is your school provided with sufficient or insufficient apparatus, or wholly without apparatus? — *Wholly without*
25. Have you an ample supply of good water for your school? — *Yes (if stock is kept out of it.)*
26. How many water closets? In what condition? — *None (Except provided by nature)*
27. What means of ventilation? — *Door, windows, cracks and Knot-holes.*
28. What are the length and breadth of school-room? — *L - 20 ft. B - 14 ft.*
29. What is the height of the ceiling? — *Ten feet*

S.L. WARD, SANTA MARIA'S FIRST SCHOOL TEACHER penned this required annual report to the County School Superintendent in 1882. His answer to school conditions question, "What means of ventilation?" was "Door, Windows, Cracks and Knot-holes".

THE "NEW" BALLENA SCHOOLHOUSE ABOUT 1886. IT COST $1,200. Girls rode side-saddle to school. Trustee Sam Warnock is shown in door way.

THE "1888 SCHOOLHOUSE" WAS THE FIRST BUILT IN THE NUEVO (RAMONA) TOWNSITE AREA.

By August 1885, the citizens of Ballena decided to do something to improve those conditions and voted 12 to 6 for a bond tax to build a new school. The amount of the bonds issued was $1,200, bearing interest at 8%.

Old timers, such as Louis Stockton who attended the first Santa Maria Valley school built on the rock pile near the road to Julian in the early 80s, remembered it as the "old rock school".

Louis was interviewed by Edgar F. Hastings in 1958 and recalled how the Stockton children rode to school every day in the family's spring wagon all the way from San Vicente Valley, (the family farmhouse was located near where Wikiup Road and Republican Way now meet). He remembered his first Ramona teacher as being Mr. Ward.

Records do indeed confirm that S.L. Ward taught the first class at that first Santa Maria Valley school. The student body averaged 13 for that year starting October 1881 and ending May 1882. Ward, hiring in as the district's first employee, was paid $58.48 per month for nine months work. For the 1882-83 year, his salary was increased to $65 per month. He didn't stay in teaching very long, for by 1886, he was working as the surveyor for the Santa Maria Land and Water Company. Thus Ward, not only was Ramona's first school teacher, but also became its first resident land surveyor.

During the 1880s and 90s such teachers were paid $65 to $75. Room and board was provided at a local home or the Adams House Hotel or Ramona Hotel, and cost them $2.50 per week, which included horse transportation to and from work.

Ramona's first school district, which in effect was that "old rock school", started with a grand total of 10 volumes in the school's library. By 1890 the library had grown to 185 volumes but the building burned down that year. It was replaced with a new structure located on land donated by the Stokes family near the old Stokes home, east of the present Magnolia Avenue on Schoolhouse Road. What happened to the library they had worked eight years to build? No account has been found. They probably had to start all over again from scratch.

The standard school day in those times was nine to four, with twenty minute recesses mornings and afternoons and a lunch hour. Children were called to class by the teacher ringing a hand bell. The 'Course of Study' was sent from the County Superintendent's office and outlined material to be covered by each grade. Children were promoted at the teacher's discretion.

The school day usually began with the singing of a patriotic song such as "America", "Red, White and Blue" or "Battle Hymn of the Republic". Other favorites were "Wait for the Wagon", "My Old Kentucky Home" and "Juanita".

Ramona didn't have its second schoolhouse until 1886, when the Spring Hill Grammar School was built. This was located in the southern part of the valley near Dye Road and Duraznitos Springs. A second Spring Hill school was built on the Rotanzi ranch in 1897 (near where the present road to Lake Sutherland meets Highway 78). That school lasted until 1943 when the district was taken into the Ramona Union District.

In 1886 the Rancho Viego Grammar School was built 3 miles north of town center near the road to Escondido. It was attended mainly by children from Clevenger, John, Howe and Pope families. It was discontinued in 1895.

Ramona Grammar School was organized in 1888. For those times, a rather handsome and substantial building was provided. Donated by the Santa Maria Land and Water Company, it was made of red brick. Before this era ended, Ramona had four such schools scattered around the townsite.

MONTICITO SCHOOL TEACHER MISS MIMIE PEASE, 1895-96. Shown in buggy with William Stockton. District furnished transportation between school and Adams House where teachers boarded.

THE EARL SCHOOL AT SOUTH END OF SANTA MARIA VALLEY. Earl was Mrs. Etcheverry's maiden name. The building is still standing, sans bell, at the north end of Mussey Grade Road.

The Earl School District was formed in 1889 to serve the children living on lands still owned by Etcheverry outside the Ramona Townsite. The district was named for Etcheverry's wife Louise, whose maiden name was Earl. The first building in this district was a little whitewashed board affair which didn't last long. It was replaced in 1896 with a new one located at the top on the Mussey Grade Road where it still stands today. Two of Ramona's leading citizens, Clara Keyes Graham and Olive Elder Peirce began long careers in their service to Ramona as teachers in that Earl one room schoolhouse.

Before the one room schoolhouse era was over and unification took place, there were thirteen such buildings scattered around Ramona, plus two in the Ballena-Littlepage area.

The first unification of school districts occurred in 1921 when the Ramona and Santa Maria grammar school districts formed the Union District. The Earl District followed in 1925. Up until then, children either furnished their own transportation to school or walked. When the two districts were unified, it was agreed that free transportation should be furnished those children living beyond walking distance. The first Ramona School bus was driven by a Mr. Lord for the Santa Maria district and a second bus was soon serving the Earl Area.

In 1943 the Spring Hill District was the last to enter the Ramona Union Grammar School District, which expanded that district to over 150 square miles.

Ramona's First High School

Early in 1894, a few of the valley's more progressive citizens, concerned that the few grammar school graduates who wished to continue their education had to go elsewhere for high school, formed the Ramona High School

TWO OF RAMONA'S FIRST HIGH SCHOOL PUPILS FLANK THE TOWN'S FIRST SCHOOL SUPERINTENDENT. Shown in later years (about 1946) are Ida Telford Barger and Rollin Peirce with John Wilson (center). The Telford and Peirce families came to Nuevo in the early 1890s when Ida and Rollin were children. They were among Ramona's first high school students.

District. Each of the valley's five grammar districts comprised the new high school district, and each was represented on its board. The first board of trustees were Isaac Green, Lillian Ross, Levi Zimmer, Thomas Jerman, Elmer Maydole, Frank Creelman and John Clevenger.

High school opened for the first time in Sept, 1894 in the upstairs loft of the Town Hall. Augustus Barnett had provided a room, (in effect, another one room schoolhouse) in his plans on the top floor for this purpose. But learning mathematics and history under those rafters was sometimes less than comfortable. In September and October it could get very hot up there and school was held downstairs in the main hall on such days. School hours were held from 9am to noon and from 1pm to 4pm. The first class at RHS numbered less that 20 students. The first principal was Wheeler J. Bailey who served only three months, when he was elected Superintendent of Schools for the County. First high school commencement was held in 1897.

8

Start of a New Town

The 1880s saw the beginning of a new town in the Santa Maria Valley. Population for the whole of San Diego county was only 8,600 at the start of that decade, and the sparsely populated valley was still primarily grazing land. Before the end of the 1880s, however, San Diego had experienced a great land boom, only to be followed by a bust. But the back country saw new towns springing up in the more desirable parts of the region.

Bernard Etcheverry

By 1881, Bernard Etcheverry was running 12,000 sheep on his 16,700-acre Santa Maria spread. But more importantly, the many orchards, vineyards, barley and wheat fields that were springing up all over his land were testimony to the more diverse agricultural potential of the valley.

Etcheverry was a native of Cambo, France who in 1856, at age 19, sailed around Cape Horn for the California gold fields. After spending three years panning gold in Colum-

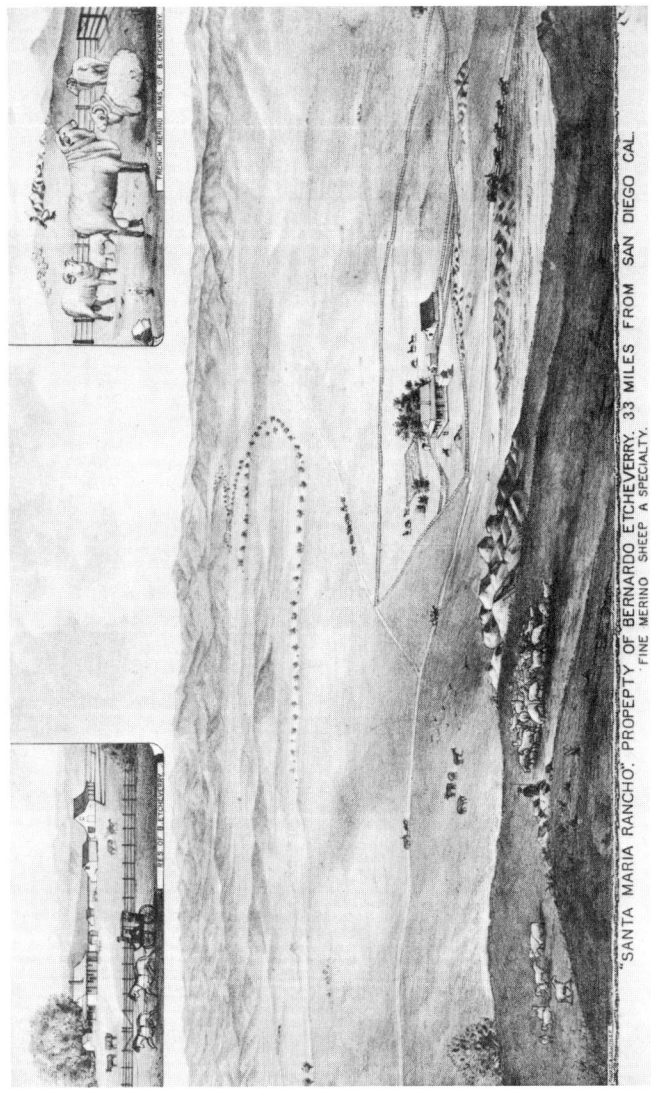

THE BERNARD ETCHEVERRY RANCH IN 1882. By then Etcheverry had acquired all the Santa Maria Rancho except 1,000 acres, and had turned the valley floor into a sea of grazing sheep, orchards and grain fields by the time this drawing was made.

W.M OSTROGA   MENTON & TROUVILLE

BERNARD ETCHEVERRY with wife Louise Earl and four young
children in Europe, summer 1885.

bia, with some degree of luck, he moved on to Santa Barbara, then back to France for a short visit before finally
settling in San Diego County in 1872.

In 1872 an associate of Etcheverry's, Juan B. Arrambide,
purchased all but 1,000 acres of the Santa Maria Rancho.
The San Diego Union later noted on July 14, 1874 that
Arrambide and Etcheverry "have fine merino rams for sale
at the Santa Maria Rancho." No record has been found as
to what the arrangement or relationship was between Arrambide and Etcheverry, but one obviously existed, for in

October 1878, Arrambide deeded one half of the ranch to Etcheverry for only $1. Less that two years later, he sold the other half to Bernard for $12,250, and Etcheverry had full possession of all 16,700 acres.

He employed up to 50 men to shear his fine marino sheep. In order to keep all these men on the job, he paid them in metal script which he exchanged for gold coin at the end of the spring wool clip. In 1883, wool production ran to 75,000 pounds.

Etcheverry is credited with having developed the first modern, progressive farming operation in the Santa Maria Valley. He encouraged share-croppers to set up homes and farms on his broad ranch and was said to be a generous landlord.

Doctor Woodson

About the time Etcheverry was starting to turn the Santa Maria Valley floor into a sea of grazing sheep and crop fields, Dr. M.C. Woodson laid claim in 1875 to 160 acres of land just south of the grant line.

Woodson was from Kentucky and had served with the Confederate Army as a dentist. He continued to practice dentistry from his modest home at the foot of the mountain which today bears his name. Those who visited his home were struck by its beautiful setting nestled in the many live oaks. He had a mixed orchard and productive garden, but what was most impressive was the immense spread of Isabella grape vines which completely covered his home.

A favorite occasion for him in later years was to gather with other local Civil War veterans in his grey uniform. All the others had fought with the Union forces, but by the 1890s this made little difference. This group of vets included Captain Green, Captain H.P. Sloane, Thomas Reynolds, Sr., Wm. Mitchell, Simon Woodward, Thomas Jerman, Wm. Miller, Louis Kunkler and I. Zimmer.

DR. M.C. WOODSON IN FRONT OF HIS HOME on the north side of the mountain that bears his name. The former Confederate Army dentist settled near the south edge of the Santa Maria Valley in 1875.

It became clear to Etcheverry by 1883, that a store was needed in the Santa Maria Valley. He persuaded a fellow Frenchman and sheep raiser, Theophile Verlaque to come up and take a look.

Verlaque had arrived in San Diego in 1870 by way of New Orleans and New Madrid, Missouri. By 1880 he had established a successful restaurant at Fifth and G, and a winery on Sixth Street and ran 2,000 sheep on the outskirts of San Diego. Verlaque and his son Amos took a look and apparently saw some business potential.

HENRY METHERELL ORCHARD AND RESIDENCE IN THE WESTERN PART OF THE VALLEY, 1882. Bernard Etcheverry encouraged farmers to settle and leased them parts of his Santa Maria Valley land. Metherell also worked for Etcheverry as ranch superintendent.

Amos purchased a two acre site that had a good spring and was located along the well beaten wagon trail to Julian. He built the Santa Maria Store and set up a postoffice on the north side of present Main Street, between sixth and seventh streets. Thus, with the establishment of this first little commercial venture in 1883 came the start of a new town named Nuevo.

Amos' brother Jeff later took over the operation and ran it for many years, renaming it the Pioneer Store. Jeff also ran the store and resort at Warner's Springs for several years around the turn of the century. Verlaque descendants owned and ran the Ramona store in that same Main Street location until 1933.

In 1886, Theophile Verlaque decided to build "a little

THE VERLAQUE GENERAL STORE AND POST OFFICE. Built in 1883, it was the first commercial establishment in Santa Maria Valley. This was the start of a new town called Nuevo, which later was renamed Ramona. The building stands today and is still being used for retail business.

THE VERLAQUE HOUSE. Today this old estate is home to the Guy B. Woodward Museum. Owned and operated for the benefit of the community by the Ramona Historical Society.

country place where he and the family might take an outing now and then from their place in town." He was attracted to the growing community and chose a homesite next door to the store. The house he built has been described as perhaps "the only building of true provincial architecture this side of New Orleans". While the claim may or may not be true, the house is indeed a rare building, and one which deserves careful preservation. With that in mind, Mrs. Stanley Ransom bought the house in 1962. Through the generosity of the Ransom family, it was donated to the Ramona Pioneer Historical Society in 1984 to be used as a museum. As a result of careful planning and much hard work on the part of Guy and Geneva Woodward and many other society volunteers, the buildings and grounds have been developed into a first rate exhibit of early Santa Maria and Ballena life.

Augustus Barnett

Another who made a big impact on the development of the young community was Augustus Barnett. Barnett was born in New York state in 1817, and so was in his senior years when deciding to settle in the Nuevo area. His was one of those first families who came west on the new transcontinental railroad, shortly after the "Golden Spike" was driven at Promontory Point, Utah in 1869.

Upon reaching the west coast, the family settled in San Jose, but moved south to San Diego five years later in search of better climate. After spending two years in the city, he found a piece of land situated between the Santa Maria and San Vicente grant lines and filed for a homestead about 1880. He subsequently added more land in and near San Vicente Valley, until 1887 when Barnett's "El Rancherea", as he liked to call it, ultimately contained over 1,300 acres. The large Barnett adobe ranch house with its 13 foot ceilings and wide verandas, stands today, much as it did in 1885 when built. Today, Augustus' grandson James Barnett lives in the house and runs the ranch which still contains over 900 acres.

Although Augustus Barnett made most of his money in the field of finance, he gained respect locally as a progressive farmer, and one of the area's largest producers of honey.

Subdivision of theValley

Etcheverry had shown that the small farmer could do very well in the Santa Maria Valley. He also had been instrumental in encouraging a commercial start in that valley with the establishment of the first retail operation and a post office proclaiming the existance of Nuevo.

Land development fever had taken hold of San Diego County by 1886. More people were coming to California with dreams of owning a small plot of ground in an environment with good year-round climate.

On the Rancho Rincon del Diablo, the Escondido Land and Town Company laid out a new town and offered small farms for sale. The same was being done by the El Cajon Valley Company, while at Rancho Penasquitos subdividers were offering 10 acre parcels for $250 each. Santa Maria was obviously ripe for subdivision.

A group of investors, headed by Los Angeles engineer and land promoter Milton Santee came to Nuevo in 1886 and liked what they saw. In June that year, Etcheverry sold Santee 3,855 acres for $31,472 or $8.16 per acre. In August the Santa Maria Land and Water Company was incorporated and capitalized at $100,000, with $92,000 already subscribed on the filing date. Incorporators of the company were Santee, president; W.H. Goucher and Thomas Fessenden from Los Angeles; R.A. Thomas from San Diego and Julius Finch of San Francisco.

The company had surveyed the land, drawn up sub-

FRIDAY MORNING, MARCH 4, 1887.

REAL ESTATE

RAMONA!

Santa Maria Ranche.

San Diego County, Cal.

The Gem Ranche of San Diego County—Pure Water—Pure Air—Fine Seminary — Good Hotel — Finest Vineyard Soil in Southern California, and the Choicest Spot for Deciduous Fruits.

THE RANCHE.

The Santa Maria Land and Water Company have subdivided and now offer for sale 7,000 acres of the choicest land in San Diego county.

RAMONA.

In the center of the tract a town has been laid out and called Ramona, and a Postoffice established thereon, the name of Nuevo Postoffice having been changed to Ramona by order of the Postoffice Department. Ramona is thirty miles from San Diego, on the line of the proposed extension of the Southern Pacific Railroad from Dos Palmas to San Diego, and the line of the proposed extension of California Southern from Oceanside. The present means of communication is by a daily line of four-horse Concord coaches.

RAINFALL.

The advantage of this Colony above all others established in San Diego county is that it lies upon the second rain belt of the county, which has an average of double the rainfall of any part of the Coast counties, and in dry years is always certain to produce full crops.

CLIMATE.

Ramona is situated 1,800 feet above the sea level, 25 miles from the Coast and above the line of fog; no dew falls, so that the air both during the day and night is absolutely free from dampness. One may sleep upon the ground in open air without the slightest fear of contracting a cold. No place in the country is there so perfectly protected a spot from ocean fogs. Asthma sufferers here find a perfect relief from their terrible suffering, and if there is a cure for consumption or bronchial complaints, it is to be found here.

WATER AND SOIL.

Cold, sparkling springs of soft granite water abound, while well water can be obtained at not more than 25 feet on any portion of the tract. In addition, we have a water right to Santa Maria Creek that will be piped to the town of Ramona, thus insuring an ample water supply at all times and all seasons. The soil is that rich, red loam so highly prized by the wine-makers of Napa and Sonoma counties. This, in connection with the fact that no irrigation is needed, makes it one of the choicest spots in California for vineyards.

The elevation of Santa Maria gives it an advantage over the lowlands in summer climate, and also in the raising of deciduous fruits, and all other products which along the Coast are deficient in that flavor peculiar to the East.

ADVANTAGES.

The University of Southern California will build and establish a Seminary in the town of Ramona that is this time will within a high place among the educational institutions of the country. Buildings costing $50,000 are to be erected on the site selected on an eminence overlooking the valley. The Seminary is endowed with ample funds for its support. Work to commence in six months. Hence those unfortunate, suffering with pulmonary and other afflictions having families, have the assurance that not only will they get relief from their troubles, but their families will not be deprived of cultured associations by making their homes here.

A fine hotel, now being constructed, will be conducted in a homelike manner and at reasonable rates, affording ample accommodations to those who wish to view the ranche and remain to test the climate and satisfy themselves of the desirability of Ramona as a home for

Health, Education, Pleasure and Profit.

All purchasers of land in the ranche or lots in the town of Ramona will be transported free of charge from San Diego to Ramona and return.

PRICE.

Lots, 50x140 feet, 20-foot alleys; single-streets, 80-foot alleys.
Main street, 100 feet wide; other streets 80 feet wide.
Price of lots on Main street, $100; corner, $200; other streets, $50; corners on other streets, $100.
Five, ten, twenty and forty-acre tracts at $20 to $50 per acre.
TERMS: One-third cash; balance in one and two years, with interest at seven per cent per annum on deferred payments. Five per cent off for cash.
For maps and information, call on or address

SANTA MARIA LAND AND WATER CO.,

MILTON SANTEE,
President and Manager,
964 Fifth St., San Diego.

DIRECTORS.	OFFICERS.
MILTON SANTEE,	MILTON SANTEE, President.
WM. H. GOUCHER,	W. H. GOUCHER, Vice-President.
THOS. FESSENDEN,	R. A. THOMAS, Treasurer.
R. A. THOMAS,	N. G. DOW, Secretary.
LEVI CHASE.	

ADVERTISEMENT APPEARING IN THE SAN DIEGO UNION, March 4, 1887. The Santa Maria Land and Water Company had subdivided over 3,800 acres of valley land and proposed that Nuevo be renamed Ramona. Lots on Main Street 100 feet wide were offered for $100, 80 ft. lots on other streets were priced at $50. Five, 10, 20 and 40 acre tracts were priced from $20 to $50 per acre. "Terms: one-third cash, balance in one and two years with interest at 7%.

division plats and was ready to sell land less than seven months later, (no planning departments, environmental impact reports nor community planning groups to get in the way of progress in those days!). An ad appeared in the March 4, 1887 San Diego Union extolling the boundless virtues of the "Santa Maria Ranche." Why rancho was spelled 'ranche' throughout the ad is hard to explain. It was they said, "The Gem Ranche of San Diego County - Pure Water - Pure Air - Fine Seminary - Good Hotel - Finest Vineyard Soil in Southern California, and the choicest Spot for Deciduous Fruits."

Potential buyers were told Ramona would soon be "on the line of the proposed extension of the Southern Railroad from Dos Palmas to San Diego, and the proposed extension of the California Southern from Oceanside." The promoters went on to say, "The University of Southern California will build and establish a Seminar in the town of Ramona that in time will attain a high place among the educational institutions of the country. Buildings costing $50,000 are to be erected on the site selected on an eminence overlooking the valley. The seminary is endowed with ample funds for its support. Work to commence in six months. Hence those unfortunates, suffering with pulmonary and other afflictions having families, have the assurance that not only will they get relief from their troubles, but their families will not be deprived of cultured associations by making their homes here."

Lots 50 by 140 feet with 20 foot alleys were priced at $100 on Main Street and at $50 on other streets. Five-, 10-, 20- and 40-acre tracts were priced at $20 to $50 per acre. "TERMS: One-third cash; balance in one and two years, with interest at seven percent per annum on deferred payments. Five percent off for cash."

The railroads never made it to Ramona, nor was the grand seminary ever built, the promoters of Escondido

Town snagged it before it could get up the hill, but the people came anyway. In time all the land sold, although it took over 25 years, what with the land bust of 1889, the depression of 1892 and other ups and downs

Santee built the promised hotel and named it, naturally, the Ramona Hotel. It was later expanded and renamed the Kennelworth Inn. He also petitioned for the postoffice to be renamed from Nuevo to Ramona, but found to his dismay that the name had already been spoken for. Helen Hunt Jackson's best selling book about the Indian maiden Ramona and her lover Alisandro was then capturing the hearts of all America. A Los Angeles County land promoter had seen the marketing possibilities and put in his claim for the name with the Post Office Department first. Never mind that the setting of the romantic novel was in San Diego County, and that it wasn't fair for some L.A. land promoter to steal the name, Milton was out of luck. The SML&WC had a land project named Ramona, but the town's official name would remain Nuevo.

If the town had its beginning in 1887 with the start of land sales by the SML&WC, it would be fair to assume that its first citizens were those living there that year. The San Diego County Directory for 1887 lists a total of 10 resident households in Nuevo: Aikin, Hal - Physician; Etcheverry, B.- Stockman; Fessenden, Geo.- Painter; Holton, Q.A.R.- Physician; McIntosh, D.- Stationkeeper; Nicholson, D.A.- Blacksmith; Santee, Milton - Hotelkeeper; Stokes, Adolfo - Stockman; Verlaque, A.J.-General merchandise and Ward, S.L. - Surveyor. There obviously were other settlers in Nuevo who were not listed in that directory, apparently because they had no professional or property status. In any event, the aspiring town was sparsely settled, and it took several years before land sales brought in enough settlers to cause Nuevo or "Ramona" to develop into more than just a one horse town.

9

The People Came

Few people who experienced those times thought of the last decade of the 19th century as the 'gay 90s'. Its been said that the label came out of the depression of the 1930 s, applied mainly by those city people looking back to the times when life was simpler and more predictable. Life in the back country in the early nineties was hard and far from predictable, what with the effects of a national depression and a local drought. But while life in the back country in those days was not especially gay, it wasn't all grey either.

Generally speaking, Ramona folks were not considered affluent, but they weren't poor. The 1890s found a new town populated by people looking for a new start. A town where most families were able to produce their own essential food needs and somehow find ways of generating a bit of spending cash as well.

According to Rollin Peirce, Ramona historian and pioneer, writing in a 1962 edition of the Sentinel, "there was plenty of wood for cutting and quail and rabbits for hunting".

Most of those settlers of the 90s had bought subdivided land from the Santa Maria Land and Water Company. Peirce recalled his parents being lured to Nuevo by the promoters' glowing advertisement. They left the town of Providence in the cold state of Iowa in November 1892, packing their family of five and travelling by rail all the way to Foster's station. The trip took five days. Rollin's father was in poor health and was able to enjoy but one California winter before passing away. They bought 100 acres, and with "fair equipment and tools", tilled the soil raising hay and grain. They produced nearly all their food and sold some produce for cash.

"Anyway there was no hunger or real poverty on these little ranches, seldom any serious illness or disease." Peirce recalled, "The only physician then, had to farm some himself."

The period from 1880, when the Santa Maria Valley counted less than a dozen white families, to 1900 when the census recorded over 115 households, was a time when the town of Ramona began to take shape. Most of that growth occurred during the decade of the 90s, after the Santa Maria Land and Water Company had been promoting their subdivision for a few years.

The Town Hall and Library

By 1893, it became apparent that Nuevo needed a town hall, a community center where citizens could congregate and where a public library could be established. At least it was apparent to Augustus Barnett, and he decided to do something about it. He talked it over with Milton Santee and other SML&WC directors who agreed to donate the necessary land for such a structure. He hired William Hebbard, a prominent San Diego architect to design the building and draw up plans.

What Andrew Carnegie later did for hundreds of small

TOWN HALL, WAS THE CENTER OF ACTIVITY DURING THIS "BACK COUNTRY DAY" CELEBRATION IN 1914. Martha and Augustus Barnett donated the building to the town in 1894 for use as a permanent library and meeting place. The west room on Main Street was for the public library. The east rooms could be rented out in order to generate income for the public facilities.

towns around the nation, Martha and Augustus Barnett did for the Santa Maria Valley a decade earlier. For while one main purpose of the Town Hall was to provide a meeting place, the Barnetts envisioned the establishment of the town's first public library. The west room facing Main Street was set aside expressly for that purpose. While construction progressed, newspapers carried requests for the donation of books and periodical subscriptions. By the time the building was finished, about 3,000 volumes had been received. Ramona's first main library room was 25 x 40 feet, plus a small reading room 10 x 25 feet.

The Town Hall was built with 16 inch adobe blocks. The walls measure 22 inches thick, after a pressed brick veneer was added. The main hall is 80 feet long and 40 feet wide. The building was said to have cost the Barnetts $10,000, a princely sum in those days. The grounds upon which the hall stands consists of two city lots totaling 100 feet of frontage.

On February 19, 1894, with construction completed, the Barnetts deeded the hall to the community and a grand dedication party was held on Washington's birthday three days later. The party lasted all night and well into the next morning with babies sleeping on the floor and horses pawing the ground outside. Barnett formed a board of trustees of close personal friends consisting of George Telford, Thomas Jerman, Irving Winnek, Jeff Verlaque and Edward Foreman to administer a deed of trust he drew up for the town hall.

While he wanted the youngsters, and young at heart, to have a place to party and dance, Barnett, the teetotaler placed a covenant in the deed that forbad the consumption of alcoholic beverages on the premises, a restriction that stands today.

Over the nearly 100 years the building has stood, it has served as home for many a civic, public and commercial enterprise. The west room was to contain the permanent library, but the east room on Main Street could be rented out to defray the costs of maintenance. It served as a real estate office, Ramona's State Bank, the Municipal Court room and jail and housed the Chamber of Commerce office. During the 1930s depression, it was headquarters for the New Deal's Civilian Conservation Corps (CCC) which ran a camp in Pamo Valley.

Today the 'Old Lady' is but a shell of her former self, just barely keeping ahead of the wrecker's ball. In February 1973, Town Hall was officially declared a point of Historical Interest, thus protecting it from demolition. But it has not served a functional purpose for several years, having been closed due to structural deficiencies and high insurance costs.

A dedicated Town Hall board of trustees continues to work to restore it, but local support has lagged to the point that there are only enough funds presently to cover meager caretaker needs. County grant funds have been solicited and the trustees are hopeful their efforts will result in getting enough to faithfully restore the building to its once proud condition.

The Post Office

The first post office established in the Santa Maria Valley was established September 23, 1883 as the Nuevo post office by Amos J. Verlaque. Milton Santee and fellow promoters, were unable to change the town name to Ramona, so Nuevo remained the official name. However, the Los Angeles County development that had preempted the Ramona name closed down its post office in the spring of 1895. A group of Nuevo citizens immediately circulated a petition to claim "Ramona" for the Santa Maria Valley and mailed it off to Washington. As a result, the post office was renamed Ramona and officially recognized as such on June 18, 1895 when the U.S. Post Office Department agreed to the change. For the first twelve years of its life, however, the town was Nuevo in all County, State and Federal records.

Early day postmasters for the Santa Maria Valley and dates of their appointment are as following: Amos J.Verlaque 9/24/83, Jeff A. Verlaque 3/3/88, Thomas Jerman 7/13/97, Luther C. Janeway 4/17/15, Henry A. Miles 3/16/17, Harlan J. Woodward 11/21/18, Lyda Verlaque 1/2/28, Geo. R. Comings 5/25/28. Others who have since served in this capacity include Enoc Russell, Charles Raub, Kenneth Drown, Leonard Walker and Don McIntosh. The present Postmaster Paul Lewis has held that position since 1980.

HUNTING PARTY ON THE FRONT PORCH OF THE BARNETT HOME DURING THE 1890s. Augustus is on far left with hat pulled down over his face. He didn't like to be photographed and this is a rare picture of him. Wife Martha is sitting in the chair next to him. Others are unidentified.

Nuevo's post office was a late comer compared with Ballena's which was established 13 years earlier in July 1870. Ballena patrons, however, had to go to Witchcreek to get their mail after their office closed in 1902.

Other back country settlements having their own post offices included Sutherland from 1895 until 1903 and Almond, located in the Pamo Valley, from 1896 until 1914. But by 1938, when Witchcreek closed, all these outlying settlements were relying on Ramona for their mail.

The Santa Maria Valley got its first free rural delivery, which began with 100 families three times a week in December 1936.

Today, the Ramona post office delivers mail to nearly 10,000 households and those modern white postal trucks cover an area of approximate 75 square miles.

The Railroad That Never Came

The San Diego, Cuyamaca and Eastern Railroad was built in 1888-89 and ran from San Diego to its terminus at Foster. It's principal organizer was Robert W. Waterman, Governor of California who made a fortune from the Barstow Mine, taking $1.6 million in silver between 1880 and 1887. He was elected Lt. Governor in 1886, and succeeded Gov. Washington Bartlett upon his death in September 1887. Waterman purchased the Cuyamaca Rancho and reopened the Stonewall Mine, which turned out to be one of the richest gold producers in the Julian area.

The railroad started at the foot of N Street in San Diego and ran 23 miles through Lemon Grove, La Mesa and Lakeside, terminating at Fosters (where the San Vicente dam is presently located).

Carlyle Daley, son of one of the railroads promoters, Thomas Daley, reminisced in 1960: "What I am wondering now, and always have wondered, is how they expected to get that railroad out of Foster where it went right up to a dead end. The railroad was supposed to go through Barona Valley and up to the mine at Julian, however, they were all broke before the railroad was finished. But I don't think that there is even a locomotive today that is powerful enough to pull a train up that grade to Cuyamaca."

But the S.D.C.& E. R.R. played a big role in the dreams and expectations of the people in Ramona, Santa Ysabel and Ballena. The railroad agreed in 1892 to extend its service to these communities in return for a guarantee of $100,000 in freight earnings. Several campaigns were jointly launched by the Ramona and San Diego Chambers of Commerce to get the tracks extended into the back country.

San Diego newspapers, the Union and the Sun were replete with reports from 1892 to 1909 telling of the efforts, trials and tribulations of the back-country leaders to get the railroad up to Ramona, Santa Ysabel and Julian. But it was not to be. The railroad never earned the money its investors expected. Capital requirements and operating costs would not allow further expansion and back country guarantees either were not forthcoming or failed to impress the railroad people.

Meanwhile, Poway was also having its hopes built up for a railroad, only to have them dashed. The promoters of a Pacific Beach & La Jolla Railroad proposed running an extension through the Poway Valley up to Santa Maria and beyond. The Poway Progress ran extensive reports on the many meetings and events happening from October 1895 to October 1896 involving this proposed development.

The railroad promoters agreed to put in $150,000 in cash or land if the back country folks would pledge a subsidy of $150,000 which was to defray the railroad's expected losses during the first year of operation. They promised that the new railroad would come as close as possible to the Poway post office. The route beyond that, and location of stations, however, was vague. Despite extensive canvassing of land owners, the desired amount for the subsidy was not raised and the project died.

Ramona leaders who were active in these two frustrating efforts included T.P. Converse, Charles L. Slone, Joseph H. Kerr, L.C. Janeway, W.E. Woodward, A.B. Foster, E.B. Tilton, A.O. Reed, E.F. Bowen and H.J. Woodward. Leaders from Ballena, Julian, Santa Ysabel, and Mesa Grande who also worked on the committees included Rex Clark, George Sawday, F.A.deLuca, Samual Rotanzi, J.C. Ferguson, Cleason Ambler and E.H. Davis. Poway leaders included L.E. Kent, W.C. Hilleary, Mrs. C.C. Wattson, Mrs. K.W. Chapin, D.B. McIver, J.C. Kear and T.J. Cambron.

The line between San Diego and Fosters, however, made

JOSEPH FOSTER AS A YOUNG MAN IN 1885. Foster ran the stage line from the railroad terminal at his ranch into the back country for many years.

FOSTER DEPOT, the eastern terminus for the San Diego Eastern and Cuyamaca Railroad as it was in 1911. Foster is located just south of where the San Vicente Dam now stands. Stage coaches furnished the transportation from there up to Ramona, Ballena, Warner's and Julian. The Mussey Grade road ran north up through were the reservoir now is, and on into the Santa Maria valley.

OPPOSING BASEBALL TEAMS POSE TOGETHER IN 1897. The Poway squad in uniform sitting and the Ramona team standing. While the two teams fought it out on the ball diamond, their town leaders worked hard together to try and get a railroad into the back country.

THE ADAMS HOUSE. One of Ramona's two hostelries. Located across the street from the Verlaque house, it catered to the traveller as well as serving as a home for many a one-room school teacher.

it possible for Ramonans to get to the city and back in one day. This required getting out by five o'clock in the morning to catch the stage down the Mussey grade. Round trip fare, stage and train, Ramona to San Diego was $4.00, and one way $2.25.

Travellers going all the way to Julian paid $3.25 one way and $6.00 round trip. This covered the 25.2 mile rail trip between San Diego and Fosters and the 34 mile stage run between Foster and Julian, via Ramona, Ballena, Witch Creek, Santa Ysabel and Wynola. There was also a stage connection at Ramona for Warner Ranch Hot Springs via a road which went through Santa Teresa, Sutherland and Mesa Grande.

A promotional pamphlet published by the railroad in the late '90s, "Mountains and Valleys" extolled the back country with "Hints and glimpses of their Scenery, Products and Possibilities, and their Pleasures and profits for Tourist and Settler *** As seen along the line of the Cuyamaca Railroad and beyond." Ramona is described as "a pretty little village, queen of the Santa Maria valley, which is rich in sleek, fat cattle and agricultural and horticultural products. " Those going to Warner Hot Springs, "the last home of the despised Indian" could also go through Santa Ysabel and stay over night in a "homelike, hospitable inn, whose welcome finds ready response from weary and hungry travelers. A splendid supper, a comfortable, clean bed and a hearty breakfast" were furnished by Moretti & Mattei, proprietors, for $1.50 per day.

The little railroad station at Fosters was a beehive of activity from daylight till dark. Foster, known as "Uncle Joe", was a partner with Frank Frary of San Diego. They organized the daily mail and passenger service using old Concord style stages.

These Concords were of special, sturdy hand-made construction; three seats inside under cover seating nine or ten

WARNER'S SPRINGS ABOUT 1903. Not the POSH resort we know today, but a resort never the less. Pictured are stage line operator Joe Foster and wife Mattie on left, and resort operator Jeff Velaque and wife Kate on the right. Verlaque ran both this and his Ramona store for about five years. People came by rail and stage from afar to enjoy the recuperative benefits of the hot springs.

persons; one at rear on top for two or three and a choice front seat with the driver back of and above the horses. The baggage and mail compartment was under canvas at the rear. Another special feature was the old-time "springs" substitute made up of 15 or 16 ply of extra heavy cow-hide leather four inches wide by about 12 feet long held at both ends with iron clamps. the coach rested and rocked on two of these leather runners with a rocking chair and roller coaster effect when going over the usually rough roads.

As described by Rollin Peirce,"The old narrow wagon road up the Mussey Grade was like an ant trail, frequented with the old Concord Stage and its prancing four horses, together with the numerous 2-4 and 6-horse drawn freight wagons plying slowly between Fosters and the mountain

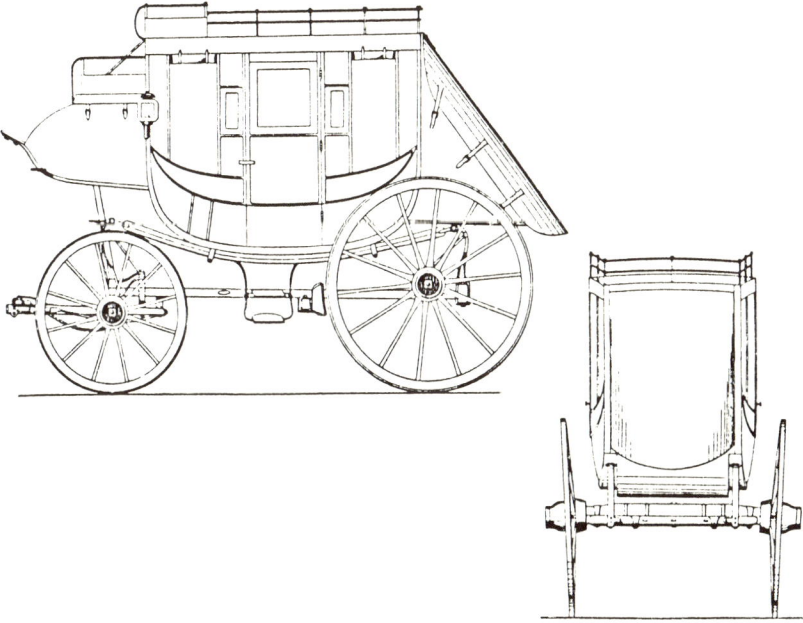

settlements with hay, grain, wool, oak wood and other products on the down trip, returning with food, mining and ranch supplies. The big teams were usually fitted out with small bells attached to the harness collar giving a warning sound that they were coming just around the corner of the numerous short bends in the road. A sharp lookout was kept for the mail stage which according to custom had the right-of-way, the teams dodging into the numerous passing pockets along the narrow roadway."

"The rollicking old Concord stage," wrote Peirce, "with its now tired out and panting four steeds having galloped most of the way up the grade and all the distance from the top into Ramona, the driver cracking his whip with foot on the old time brakes sliding the wheels, the foaming restless horses were soon to be relieved with a fresh set of ours at the halfway stage station three miles east, a little beyond or above the old McIntosh home on the old Julian-Ballena road." This station was managed by James Booth, father of Elmer. He always had four fresh horses harnessed and ready to go for both the up and down trips as the coaches arrived. The stage station was abandoned in 1912 when the autos took over.

Uncle Joe Foster

When Governor George C. Pardee named Joseph Foster to be San Diego County's 3rd district supervisor in February 1906,   replacing James Jasper, he may not have foreseen how effective and honest a public servant he was appointing. As it turned out, Foster served 23 years as a member of the board of supervisors and as chairman of that body for over half his tenure. He was a constant champion for better back country roads and has been credited with development of Highway 78. By the time he retired from the board, most of the county employees, as well as his many constituents called him "Uncle Joe" as if he were one of their own family.

Foster operated the stage and mail service between Julian and the railhead named for him. After 30 years of continuous service, he retired his four-horse stage service in 1914 when automobiles started taking over. Fred P. Frary, former mayor of San Diego, was his partner in business for 10 of those years.

Joe Foster was born in Sacramento in 1857 and moved to San Diego County when he was 12 years old. He married Martha Swycaffer, daughter of Ballena's early pioneer, Joe Swycaffer in 1880. The newlyweds moved to his small ranch, located where the San Vicente dam is today. They ranched there together until Uncle Joe died in 1933.

The San Diego Cuyamaca and Eastern Railroad terminal was located on their ranch. The rails reached Foster in 1889 and Joe and Martha were very much involved in that beehive of activity until the great flood of 1916 washed out the roadbed above Santee, never to be replaced.

10

Gemstones & Minerals

Much has been written about gold in San Diego County. The Julian boom which began in 1870 provided the driving force for development and commerce along the back country trails winding between that mining town and San Diego. But as the century came to an end, those mines had pretty well played out.

Gold, however, was not the only glitter that proved profitable in these country hills. Starting in the early 1890s, a relatively secretive and little known industry was developing here in rare gemstones. The value of rare gems taken from San Diego County during the first decade of this century has been estimated to exceed $2 million (in 1911 dollars), a sum equal to half of all the gold ever mined in Julian. This was over a relatively short period of time.

Prior to the overthrow of the Chinese Manchus dynasty in 1911, mines near Ramona, in Mesa Grande and Pala were furnishing much of the tourmaline that was so highly prized by the "Last Emperor's" family.

Few gemstones intrigue the mineral collector so much as

the tourmaline. It can display a surprising array and range of color. Sometimes as many as four or five distinct hues are seen in a single crystal.

Various stories have been told about how this gemstone first came to light in San Diego County. One is that Indian children, along with Angel family children playing in the Mesa Grande area in the early-1890s, picked up oddly shaped six-sided quartz crystals, about three inches long and a little thicker than a lead pencil. Upon cleaning them, they were found to be beautifully colored, light blue and partially clear. The white cattlemen and prospectors showed little interest since the stones weren't gold, nor did they look like diamonds. It was, however, later recognized as tourmaline by those who understood its value. Further digging revealed pink tourmaline as well, which had long been a favorite of the Chinese to whom it has religious significance.

Many other varieties of gemstones have been found near Ramona, including even diamonds, although that find consisted of mere traces in the flats below Little Three Mine on Hatfield Creek in the early 1900s.

According to Elbert "Mac" McMacken, long time Ramona resident, gemologist and miner, "San Diego County's hills contain a greater variety of gemstones than any area its size in the world." But it was the tourmaline, kunzite, beryl, topaz and garnet that have been mined with the most financial success in the Ramona area off and on for nearly 100 years.

What is it that makes this part of San Diego County so rich in gemstones? Briefly, it is due to an accident of nature. When the mountains of Southern California were formed in this area, a tremendous upwelling of molten rock thrust its way to the surface like an enormous blister, and when it solidified , it formed the beginning of what is known as the Southern California Batholith.

The Himalaya

Approximately 90 percent of the gem and near-gem quality tourmaline coming from Southern California came from but five mines. Two in the Mesa Grande area, and three in the Pala district.

One of these, and perhaps the most successful of gemstone operations has been the Himalaya Mine located in Mesa Grande. It is today, the largest gem producer in North America and recently the longest running in contiuous operations, more than 20 years.

The Himalaya was officially located and staked out in 1898 by prospector Gail Lewis. Serious mining for tourmaline started later that year. This mine proved to be such an immediate and fabulous success that in 1902, Tiffany's of New York directed its agent J. Lippman Tannenbaum to make a grab for it. Using an intermediary, who posed as a tuberculosis sufferer, Tannenbaum bought the Lewis' homestead for a pitance and claim-jumped the Himalaya. By 1904, the mine had yielded 6 tons of tourmaline and the new owners were doing a thriving business with Tzu Hsi, dowager empress of China.

The other successful area producer was the adjacent San Diego Mine, which was located upon the same pegmatite body and was opened in 1901.After the initial discovery period, Mesa Grande production rose steeply until a peak was reached in 1910.

The Himalaya's onsite superintendent was J. Goodman Braye, a black man who liked to refer to himself as "The Black Millionaire." Mine foreman during those heyday years, 1902-1912 was Vance Angel, uncle of Milton Angel member of that pioneer Mesa Grande family and today an active north county grading contractor.

Tannenbaum had an arrangement with an export bank in New York which held Chinese funds to pay for the dowager empress' tourmaline purchases. The bank was instructed to pay Tannenbaum cash upon the order and shipment of gems to the empress. The story goes, according to William Larson, one of the current owners of the Himalaya, that the empress placed a large order just before she died in 1911. The order amounted to $360,000, a very large sum in those days. Tannenbaum learned of her death before the bank did, got the shipment off and collected his money before the order could be cancelled. That was to be the last large tourmaline sale made to the Manchurian Dynasty.

With the fall of the reigning empire in 1912, exports were drastically curtailed. The onset of World War I prevented further resumption of trade, while the development of Brazilian sources took most of the market formerly supplied by California mines. These factors caused the almost overnight cessation of production mining for the gem in this area.

In 1957, the Himalaya was reopened by then owner, Ralph Potter, who was accompanied by Mac McMackin and internationally reknowned gem expert Captain John Sinkankas. It had laid idle with its timbers rotting since being abruptly closed in 1912. An antiquated kerosene lamp still hung on an old prop at one side of the tunnel, confirming the oft-told tale that when Tannenbaum found his Chinese market collapsing, he telegraphed Braye to stop work immediately, pay off the crew, and close down the mine.

This expedition 45 years later, was very exciting for those gemologists. They likened the experience of running into the previously uncovered rich pockets to the opening of pirate treasure chests.

Today the Himalaya is owned by Pala International, Inc., with San Diego County gemologist and dealer William Larson one of its principal partners. The mine still yields high grade tourmaline and currently employs seven full time miners. Since 1980, according to Larson, over 7,000 feet of new underground tunnel has been dug and 24,000 pounds of tourmaline extracted.

The growing awareness for colored stones has resulted in a 10-fold increase in values since the early 1970s, when Larson first got involved in local gem mining.

Mines on Hatfield Creek

Near Ramona, and situated beside Hatfield Creek about five miles east of town, are the Little Three Mine, the ABC Mine, the Black Panther, the Hercules and the Surprise Mine all of which, with varying degrees of success, have produced gemstones over the past 90 years.

D. C. Collier was reported to have found garnets near his country home on Hatfield Creek. Up until 1941, the old road from Ramona to Ballena still forded the creek at that location and was commonly referred to as the Collier Crossing. The old Collier home sat on stilts next to this crossing, but both house and crossing have been long gone.

The Little Three Mine is the only Ramona mine being worked on a regular basis today. It is owned by Louis B. Spaulding, Jr. of Ramona, who like his father before him, has been able to extract enough gem and specimen quality blue topaz and spessartite garnet to make the mine a paying operation for the past 30 some years. The garnet, which is orange in color is quite rare and is found in only one other mine in the United States.

"The story goes," Spaulding told me, as we stood at one of Little Three's tunnel openings one recent sunny January morning, "that this gem rich hill was discovered about 1903, when Grandma McIntosh was chasing a stray cow off their ranch. She stumbled on a great big green tourmaline in the creek right below where we're standing. A friend from Escondido, (H.W. Robb) saw the specimen and recognized it for what it was. They got to prowling around on the hill

LOUIS SPAULDING, JR. AT ENTRANCE TO "LITTLE THREE MINE". The mine is one of a very few still producing gem quality stones in the United States. Located near Hatfield Creek about four miles east of Ramona, the mine is noted for its spessartite garnets.

here and found a lot of them, right on the surface. So Dan McIntosh, Robb and another fellow, Charles F. Schnack from Escondido, formed a partnership, that's where the "Little Three" name came from. They bought this 40 acres from John Ferguson and proceeded to go to work. They really didn't have too much luck, other than hitting one tremendous pocket of Topaz in 1905."

As was the case with other pegmatite gem mines in San Diego county, mining activity came to a halt in 1912. Only sporatic high-grading took place until the Spauldings started to work the mine regularly in 1955.

Ramona native George Ashley, and renown gemstone expert, wrote in 1966 about his experience with mining in the Ramona area. "The best mines in the Ramona area were the Little Three and the ABC gem mines." Ashley recalled. "The Little Three had the only pocket of pink - really more of a salmon shade - toumaline. It produced about 100 pounds of blue topaz, also green tourmaline and spessartite garnet. The ABC produced a substantial quantity of pink beryl and some essonite garnet."

Both Ashley and Guy Woodward recall as youngsters, during the early 1920s, walking up Hatfield Creek and finding gem remnants in mine tailings along the creek. The boom years, from about 1903 to 1912, were long gone, but their past was still very much in evidence.

The senior Spaulding and his father in law, former Sentinel publisher C.A. Seay, according to Lou Jr. "had always been interested in gem mining around here and got hold of the old ABC about 1924. They hit one pocket of garnets that was pretty nice. But apparently it was the only pocket that was easy to get to, so they sold the property."

Louis Sr., besides farming and mining, was Ramona's official weather observer for nearly 25 years, from 1949 until he died in 1973. Since that time, the Ramona Fire Department has assumed the responsibility for weather reporting for the area.

Tumbled gems

Ramona is home to one of the world's largest producers of tumbler-polished gems. Craftstones is the name of the firm and it has been run by Herb and Mary Walters since 1953. Not all the stones the Walters polish and distribute are considered precious but they attract a wide market never the less.

Among the raw material the company buys and polishes are magnasite, coral, aveturine, ruby, citrine, sapphire, quartz, garnet, amethyst, agate, mother of pearl, rhodonite, rock crystal, lapis lazurlia, emerald and jade. Chunks of material ranging from three inches in diameter to boulder size arrive at the Craftstone plant. The larger ones have to be broken down to sizes that the tumbler machines can handle. The tumbling effect of the machines is similar to that which a stone would get in a rapid running stream bed. Water and abrasives are added and the machines run three to four weeks at a time, day in and day out. After sorting, grading, resorting and repolishing, the finished product is ready for the market.

Polished stones are sold world-wide in large quantities to wholesalers.

The Elm Avenue factory has enough processing capacity to handle 400,000 pounds of raw material to produce 200,000 pounds of finished product. The Walters employ over 20 in Ramona and operate another plant near Tijuana, Mexico.

Gold and Copper

While most history buffs equate gold in the San Diego back country with the Julian-Banner area, much excitement about the glitter has been generated around Ramona in the past as well.

Serious gold mining took place as recently as 1930 in the San Vicente Valley where expensive homes are now located in the Country Estates community. Water was pumped up from the San Vicente Creek near the present number 14 fairway on the golf course, to the side of the hill where Oak Springs Drive now meanders. High power jets of water were used to force ore bearing rock to the surface. Gravel was washed on huge rockers. But according to June Scarbery, the equipment kept breaking down. June is the daughter of John Mykrantz, who leased the land to the operators. Tailings from that effort are still very much in evidence today.

County records indicate that Ballena Placers, Inc. recorded the Mykranz mining lease in February 1926, but quitclaimed it in August 1927. San Vicente Placer Company took up the lease that same month. California State Division of mines reports show the Mykrantz land yielded but $14,500 in gold between 1924 to 1930 when operations ceased.

Klondike Creek, which crosses Wildcat Canyon road about a mile south of San Vicente road, was so named because of the gold mining that took place along its banks. Scars from hydraulic action can be detected today on the hillside bordering the creek. James Barnett, grandson of Augustus Barnett, recalls seeing rusted mining equipment lying near the creek up until World War II when it was hauled off for scrap.

The Daley Mine

A mile or two further southwest, on the old Barona ranch, now called the Monte Vista by its current owners, another kind of mining took place.

Carlyle M. Daley, son of Thomas J. Daley who bought the Barona ranch in 1885, was interviewed by Edgar F. Hastings for the San Diego Historical Society in 1960:

"After my father acquired the Barona ranch he was driving over it to see what he had. He and Johnnie Boyd found a copper blowout and they left their tools there — a pick and shovel — and came back into town. It was a month or so before they went out again. They couldn't find the location again and they never could find their pick and shovel but they discovered another blowout. This blowout — surface ore — was similar to the United Verde Mine in Jerome, Arizona, which is probably one of the most famous copper mines in the world.

"This blowout ore attracted many miners to the place

and it sold several times but never stayed sold, we always got it back. Originally it sold to the Boston and Maine Company for $100,000 and a $1,500 deposit was collected. The last time it sold was when I sold it in 1930 for $7,500 to two old men by the names of Ott and Lindsey. Lots of money was spent out there but no money at all ever taken off. The ore was pretty rich and kept getting richer all the time, however they were a long ways from water level which they would have to be before they found out whether they had a copper mine or not.

"As far as I know it is still out there - just a hole in the ground. If I remember right the main shaft is down about 130 feet and from there tunnels are drilled off."

Carlyle apparently lost track of activities at the mine after he sold it. For while the mine was not a roaring success, records show it was not a complete failure either.

In addition to the Boston and Maine Company, several other firms showed interest in the deposit, with varying degrees of success. A February 13, 1900 item in the San Diego Union reported that articles of incorporation had been filed for the Barona Copper Mining & Smelting Co. the day before. The company was formed "for the purpose of developing the large ledge of copper on the Daley Ranch" if it proves out, they added, "Eastern capitalists will buy the mine." The Union reported further on March 4th that the "sinking of a shaft began last week." Fine samples of copper were placed on display, they added, in the mining room of the San Diego Chamber of Commerce.

Between 1914 and 1919, the San Jacinto Mining & Milling Company worked the mine. Ore was smelted in a 50-ton reverbatory furnace. The total production was about 175,000 pounds of copper, of which about 150,000 was produced in 1917 when, because of Wold War I, the price of copper reached a peak of 27 cents per pound.

In 1924 George W. Lindsey purchased the property containing 100 acres, and leased it out to other operators who were unsuccessful at making it pay.

In 1935, Lindsey commissioned a rather extensive study to determine feasibility of further operation of the mine. Several geologists concluded that copper ore was no longer profitable and future success would depend upon finding consistent gold and silver values.

As an aside, one of those geologists, James R. Evans, offered the following definition in his letter: "A geologist " he said, "is a fellow who tells you where ore is to be found - and - when you don't find it - can explain in a scientific manner just why it wasn't there.

Apparently the ore wasn't there in sufficient values to justify the expense of reactivating the mine, for it has been idle since.

11

A New Century

By the turn of the twentieth century, according to the U.S. Census, the Santa Maria and San Vicente Valleys had a population of 404. The Santa Maria Land and Water Company had weathered the San Diego land bust of 1888 and the national depression of 1892-93, but still had a large inventory of unsold lots and parcels. D.C. Collier would buy them out in 1905.

There were about 116 families carving out livings in the area. Orchards, vineyards, farms, pastures and grain fields dotted the valley floors and foothills. Ramona's main street boasted a dozen or so buildings which housed enterprises bent on serving the growing community's needs while bringing in a few new dollars from the passing traveler.

On the south side of the dusty thoroughfare was 'Abels Meat Market' with adjacent hay and feed room, the livery and feed stable, Abel Adams shoe and harness shop, the small Adams House Hotel, blacksmith shop, a card and pool club and the Sentinel's office. While on the north side, the local saloon and watering trough wetted the whistles of both man and beast. Further down the north side were the Verlaque general store and post office, the Ramona Hotel, Jerman's combination paint and drug store and the Town Hall, which housed the public library as well as various business enterprises from time to time.

Firing the Anvil

The firing of anvils was a popular way of making noise to celebrate the Fourth of July or any special occasion when there was no cannon handy. From the middle of the 19th century on into the first two decades of the 20th, Californians celebrated wetly and noisily. One small-town method of creating a big bang was practiced with the town blacksmith's anvils and a liberal amount of black powder.

As described by Arthur Woodward in an article for the San Diego Historical Society, he recalled seeing and hearing as a young boy, the anvils fired on Main Street in front of Frank Creelman's blacksmith shop on Independence Day.

"The two anvils used stood on the ground in front of the open door. The largest of the anvils was placed upside down. Anvils varied in weight from small ones of ten pounds to monsters weighing around 800 pounds. However, I should judge that the ones used in the Fourth of July firing in the early 1900s in Ramona weighed 100 pounds. These instruments were made of either wrought or cast iron with steel faces; some were solid cast steel as well. The bases of these anvils were hollow in the form

of a square. Black powder, varying in amounts accord-
ing to the strength of the anvil and the explosion desired,
was poured into the bottom of the anvil on the ground.
Some anvil firers then placed a small rectangle of dam-
pened cardboard over the powder, fitting it snugly in
place, but leaving a small opening at one end directly
under the small opening at the squared end of the top
anvil (which was also placed into position upside down
and crossways) so that the small round hole in the
squared end was directly over the opening in the
cardboard beneath. Into this round hole was poured
enough black powder to form a firing train. Then the
blacksmith heated a long thin rod until it was red hot in
his forge. The men charging the anvil stood to one side,
and the sizzling iron was applied to the powder. Then
came the damndest bang you ever heard. A most satis-
fying, hell-roaring sound. The ground shook and the
upper anvil sailed into the air. The blacksmith grinned,
shifted his chaw into the side of his cheek and said:
"Pretty good, huh? Fill'er up boys and we'll do it again!"

Through the Eyes of a Country Editor

Scanning the pages of the Ramona Sentinel during those years gives one a feel for what it must have been like living in a town such as Ramona during the first part of this century.

D. N. Dodson, a salty small town journalist, was editor and proprietor of the Sentinel then and came about as close to a Mark Twain as Ramona is likely to see. He had an opinion about most happenings in and around town and didn't mince words in expressing them.

Dodson was recognized throughout San Diego County as a man with few peers when it came to first hand knowledge of real life in the old west. He learned the printer's trade at the compositor's case, as an apprentice in Fort Dodge, Iowa. Moving to Texas, he followed his trade while studying law and was admitted to the Texas bar in 1878. He practiced law in Denton, Texas for two years, and while there, served one term as that city's mayor and later served as justice of the peace of Clay County, Texas. He moved to Dallas, then San Diego and Escondido during the land boom of 1887, and on to Valdez, Alaska; all the time practicing his legal or publishing trade as opportunities and circumstances dictated. He finally came to Ramona, bought the Sentinel in 1902, and settled down.

One of the more lively controversies of that time was whether or not Ramona was to be dry. Augustus Barnett was one who advocated prohibition and was active in seeing that the local saloon be abolished. Barnett also was a progressive farmer and commercial producer of honey and one who was ever on the alert for new enterprise in the area. One such proposal was met by Dodson with the following editorial, on September 1, 1902:

"Our friend, A. Barnett, suggests that we devote some space to the encouragement of the growing industry —

the horned toad business. We are always anxious to receive suggestions from our friends especially when it relates to our material interests, but this question presents itself to the editorial mind: if all the horned toads are gathered up, will we not in time be overrun with pissants? These insects are kept from being a serious pest in our sunny southern clime by the voracious appetite of the horned toad. Ants seem to thrive best in dry places. Now if all the horned toads should all be carted off to market and Ramona should happen to go "dry" at the coming election, an invasion of the town by pissants would be inevitable. No, friend Barnett, the only condition upon which we can agree to whoop up the horned toad industry is that you shall get out and help us stamp out this prohibition heresy."

In Nov. 1904, an election was held to determine if Ramona would allow continuance of the Nuevo Saloon's license. These were the days before the State of California regulated such matters, and a liquor license was issued by the County of San Diego only if a majority of the qualified voters in the district gave approval.

Dodson wrote in the edition before the election, "With license, a man gets a drink and goes home satisfied. With prohibition, he gets a jug and gets drunk. There is many a dollar that has stopped in Ramona that would have gone on, but for our saloon. Kill it and the dollar will roll out of our reach. Save the boys by voting for license."

The next edition of the paper told of the election outcome and Dodson's opinion of it.

Headline story: 11/11/04

"Ramona Dry. — Roundheads in the Majority. — The Sentinel For Sale. — Good Chance for a Long Haired Prohibitionist to Get Into a Good Business. --

"The Sentinel gave the people some good sound advice last week on the license question. It was given in the interest of the town, not the joint. It was founded upon a profound study of the situation and an experience from residence in many towns. The people—that is, by a majority of 14—treated our advice with contempt, and voted to make Ramona dry. A more foolish town struggling to grow. The editor feels that his influence is gone and he doesn't want to publish the Sentinel any longer than he can help. We believe we have some friends among our readers, and we want to ask a favor of them. If any of you know of a pious, psalm-singing, long-haired hypocritical prohibitionist that knows anything about the newspaper business, drop him a card at our expense. Tell him the paper can be bought reasonably, that there is a rich field here, and that he will be in his element. The paper will be sold cheap, if a purchaser can be found who is brave enough to tackle it in a dry town of this size, and the editor will retire to a chicken ranch. We like this valley and many of its people. We expect to remain here, but we don't want to wear out trying to build up a town on the dry plan. The only two enterprises that bring in a cent of transient or foreign money to Ramona, outside the hotel, is the saloon and the Sentinel, but a majority of 14 "Roundheads" show that neither are appreciated. The tyranny of majorities "makes the countless thousand mourn."

"After a "dry" election to have three days of east wind, it's enough to give any man the jim-jams."

Item: 11/18/04

"The nights are getting cool and the mornings likewise. The Sentinel has a stove, as it always had, but it always wasn't "put up". Messrs. Bargar and Telford came over and put in a terra cotta chimney, arranged the stovepipe,

and now our roller, which won't work when it is still, can be warmed without carrying it out in the sun to thaw. All is serene and the editor is not as mad as he was, but we will remark incidentally that if there is anything that Johnny Bargar can't do we would like to know what it is."

Item: 2/26/1904

"It's a very poor, as well as unpatriotic man who cannot afford to contribute two cents a week to help support his home paper. That is the cost of the Sentinel-$1.00 a year."

Item: 9/9/1904

"The Sentinel has purchased the old Ober blacksmith shop and is fitting it up for a printing office. Haven't money enough to fix it up, but have plenty on the books. If you are behind on your subscription, bring in your dollar, and if you would thaw out and pay in advance, like you should do, it would be a great accommodation at this particular time. The old shop will not make a model office, but it is the only chance at present."

Item: 2 /6/1904

"Chairman Jasper of the supervisors, County Auditor Shaffer and District Attorney Carter counted the cash in the county treasury and found the balance correct at $197,632.33."

Item: 9/6/04

"Attention is called to the announcement of James A. Jasper, as a candidate for supervisor of the third district. Mr Jasper is so well known in this district, which he has served so faithfully, that nothing we could say would add to his popularity. From this writing it looks like there is nothing that could prevent Mr. Jasper's re-election.

James A. Jasper served on the San Diego County board of supervisors from 1893, when he took over this back country district from Chester Gunn. His constituency included all the territory east of Lakeside to the Colorado River, north to Riverside County and South to the Mexican border. He took great pride, according to his granddaughter Cynthia Kunkel, in making regular circuits of his vast district on horseback, seeing to it that the rude trails and roads had signs to tell the weary traveler where the next watering place was. The job paid $1,200 a year; $900 salary and $300 for horse feed.

He resigned from the board in late 1905 to become chairman of the San Diego Chamber of Commerce and helped bring that organization out of debt. He was drafted by the board of supervisors in 1907 to be publicity representative for San Diego, and traveled throughout the United States promoting the virtues of the area.

Jasper was born in Texas, and one of his earliest recollections was seeing his father go off to the Civil War as a volunteer, and returning disabled. James as the eldest child had to help support the family and was thus denied formal higher education. But he was ambitious, and educated himself through broad reading.

Jasper was one of the first owners of the Sentinel. An account of how he got involved in the newspaper business is found in another chapter of this book.

Item: 11/24/1904

"Supervisor Jasper was in Ramona Monday en route home. His friends whom he met heartily congratulated him on his re-election."

Item: 2/6/1904

"Charley Darrough gave the Sentinel a blowing up because nothing had been said about "Hotel de Klondike" — the road-worker's camp on the grade. The Sentinel doesn't know much about it, and never stopped at that hotel, but hastens to say that it is one of the best hotels he never stopped at in his life."

WITCH CREEK HOTEL WAS A POPULAR PLACE TO STAY IN THE BACK COUNTRY. Pictured here about 1907 is U.S. Grant, Jr. (far right on upper porch) and party. Cora and Clarence Wood bought this beautiful house in 1903 and converted it into an inn where many rich and famous people stayed. Covered by grape vine and wisteria, it was said that the inn never had less than 12 at the dinner table on any night. Daughter Margaret Wood Bancroft was raised here and later became a San Diego luminary. The garden at the Guy B. Woodward Museum was recently dedicated to her memory.

Item: 1/18/1904

"The Sentinel man was talking to M.A. Minor the other day. He is one of our best citizens, not intently bent on getting rich, but content to make a good living and keep a little ahead. In regards to his chickens he said that on Jan. 1st, 1903, he started in with 165 hens, that on April 1st he sold 75 of them. During the year, up to Jan. 1st, 1904 he had sold $248 worth of eggs and $70 worth of chickens. He has now on hand 216 chickens. It looks like it ought to pay."

Item: 3/11/1904

"The Ramona baseball boys went to Escondido Sun-

day and got done up as badly as they did up the San Pasqual team --23 to 2 in Escondido's favor. Guess the moon is in the wrong quarter."

Item: 12/30/1904

"*Congressman Daniels sent the Sentinel a few garden seeds. We had an item in type inviting the public to call and get them. But as they are all about gone, we won't say anything at all about them.*"

Item: 4/1/1904

"*Odie Fewell is about to put on a through stage line from Ramona to Warner. Now if a mail line can be worked up it should be done. A letter from Mesa Grande to Warner, 12 miles distant, has to travel through three counties to get to its destination.*"

Item: 7/1/1904

"*Joseph Foster has a splendid new stage on his line which he recently had made in Los Angeles at a cost of about $500.*"

Item: 4/15/1904 "

John Darrough brought from Santa Ysabel Monday 4,100 pounds of cream. We need a railroad."

For many years during that era, the paper's front page included two little boxes as part of the Sentinel flag. The one on the left proclaimed, "A railroad will stimulate development. Water will bring prosperity to all. Let us pull together and get them.", and the one on the right said, "The Sentinel will use all legitimate means in its power to hasten the advent of both propositions."

Item: 5/20/1904

"*Mr. Bargar went down to Foster Monday morning to continue the double metallic circuit on the telephone line from San Diego to Ramona. Clarence Telford, Arthur Stockton, Mr. Baxey and others from Ramona are assisting.*"

MATCH RACES DOWN MAIN STREET WERE NOT TOO UNCOMMON DURING THE EARLY PART OF THIS CENTURY. This pictures one of those horse races about 1915, and according to Fred Grand, the winning horse here was "Pando", owned by Fred's grandfather August Venoni. Verlaque house is on far right, Creelman's blacksmith shop on far left.

Item: 9/9/1904

"Mr. Bargarhas this week put in new telephones at all places on the main line from Foster to Julian and Mesa Grande,"

Item: 5/20/1904

"Dr. Case has a horse that seems to have some horse sense. Going up the grade to Mesa Grande a large rattlesnake crossed the road just as they were there. Without a moment's thought his horse jumped upon the snake and stamped the life out of him with his forefeet. After the tragedy the horse turned around and looked at the doctor as if he wished to know whether he approved of the procedure."

LA JOLLA COVE ABOUT 1906. Advertising on the bath house for "Ramona Tent Village in the Big Trees" was meant to lure the tourists up to the back country.

Item: 7/22/1904

"Messrs. Woodward and Eaton took a merry party of young ladies to the Tent Village Wednesday night to enjoy the evening on the new bowling alleys. A very nice time is reported."

The Ramona Tent Village was inspired by the success of the del Coronado Hotel's tent city on the Silver Strand. This back country retreat was located in Goose Valley where the present Town and Country Mobilehome Park is today and was built and promoted by Thomas P. Converse. It boasted such planned activities as lawn tennis, croquet, target shooting and bowling. Here was a place where the family could get away into the cool oak groves and rent a tent with wooden floor and water for $5 a week.

Item: 9/16/1904

"There is to be a horse race down in Woodward's pasture tomorrow afternoon about 2 o'clock. All are invited and some fun is expected."

RAMONA TENT VILLAGE. A place to get away for lawn tennis, bowling, croquet, target shooting and other recreation in the cool shade of the giant oaks. A tent with wooden floor and water rented for $5 a week.

Item: 10/28/1904

"The people of the mountain country are not all dead, even if we did have a dry year. The resources of this inland empire are varied. If one does not win, on account of some kind of Pluvius, we get up some other scheme and get there just the same. Jeff Verlaque had a horse that he believed was fast. Jeff Swycaffer of Julian was in the same condition. For a couple of years there was bantering, but it finally terminated in a race on Tuesday. There was a large crowd in attendance, and bets ran high, $200 changed hands in favor of Mr. Verlaque. Mr. Verlaque is "from Missouri." About $800 changed hands on the outside and it is reported that Julian will have to issue bonds to "recoup," but we believe this is a josh. There was another race that was somewhat interesting. Thomas Dye and Ed Littlepage had a lively race, $20 stakes, and Mr. Dye's horse won."

THE KENNELWORTH INN SHOWN ABOUT 1915. Originally built by Milton Santee in 1887 and called the Ramona Hotel. It was a one story building until local merchant and owner H.A. Miles built a second story to handle extra business anticipated from the 1915 Panama-Pacific Exposition. Located where the present Bank of America is, it was operated for many years by Ida May Kearney, Mark Kearney (left) and George Rouques (right). The inn was famous all over southern California and people jammed its dinning room every weekend for their renowned turkey dinners. The hotel, which had 35 rooms, burned down in 1943.

Trees on Main Street

The twentieth century was 10 years old when the citizens of Ramona decided something should be done about providing a bit more shade, as well as trying to keep down the dust on Main Street.

Mrs. Carlin Dougherty recalled in an interview with the San Diego Union in 1971, how as a little girl of eight, she and friend Frank Row, with several other young children, pulled little wagons filled with small eucalyptus and helped plant over 500 trees on Ramona's main thoroughfare. The County of San Diego furnished the seedlings and the older boys and ranchers volunteered with the post hole diggers. Two months later, however, many of those trees had died in one of the hottest summers in years. The planting process was repeated with volunteers hand-watering the young trees in order to get them established.

Some 50 to 70 years later those same trees, grown to gigantic size, have been the source of ongoing controversy. With the community of 500 having grown from horse and buggies in 1910 to over 25,000 driving cars in 1989, the two-lane Main Street that also serves as Highway 67, has become increasingly strained with traffic. The need for more travel lanes and better visibility would dictate the removal of some of these trees. As early as the 1960s it was recognized that something would have to be done. However, so far the protesters have seemed to out number the doers and debate taken precedence over action.

If there had been more planning and planting, and less protesting, a second set of trees started 25 feet back, 20 years ago, would today be as tall as the old ones planted in 1910. Its still not too late to plant.

Colonel Charlie Collier

The word Collier today is most often associated in Ramona with a pastoral park in town center which bears that name. But the man for whom the park was named was anything but retiring.

D.C. Collier was a dynamic San Diego leader, an attorney and real estate developer. His interest in parks and cultural preservation was best exemplified by the influence he had on the planning, promotion and design of the 1915-1916 Panama-California Exposition. The beautiful Spanish buildings and gardens which still stand today in Balboa Park, are very much his creation.

While most of his business interests were in San Diego, he had a love affair with the Santa Maria Valley, maintain-

COLONEL CHARLIE COLLIER (FAR RIGHT) WITH THEODORE
ROOSEVELT with Indian mother and papoose in the Indian exhibit
at the Panama-Pacific Exposition 1915. Collier considered Ramona
his home away from San Diego. He bought out the Santa Maria Land
and Water Company's inventory in 1905 and donated land for
Collier Park in Ramona in 1914. This was the county's first park.

ing a country home and spending as much time there as he
could. He organized the Ralston Realty Company in San
Diego in 1904, later renaming it D.C. Collier & Co. He also
served as lieutenant colonel on the staff of Governor J. W.
Gillett, 1907-1911, which accounted for his being referred
to as Colonel Collier by many.

Collier was the first director general of the exposition
and was instrumental in setting its theme. He endeavored
to recreate the Spanish and Mission days. He successfully
lobbied for its international recognition and was considered a power in Washington.

WORLD WAR I TROOPS ON MANEUVERS IN THE BACK COUNTRY. Shown marching down Ramona's Main Street in 1918.

Charlie Collier's interest in parks and cultural preservation extended into Ramona. In December 1914 he donated the 7.65 acres of land which became San Diego County's first park. The County agreed to finance the improvements, and the local Chamber of Commerce agreed to supervise the work. Collier, in spite of his busy schedule, was personally involved in the park's landscape design and planting in the spring of 1915.

For his many contributions to the community, he was later named an honorary life member of the Ramona Chamber of Commerce.

12

Small Town Press

Small town newspapers often reflect more the personality of their one man editor-publisher than they do the town they write about. Ramona's local paper has been no exception. It has had many colorful proprietors over the years.

On May 11, 1928, the Ramona Sentinel celebrated its 41st anniversary with a feature story about its history. Actually, it was not always known as a 'Ramona' newspaper. In fact, it didn't formally proclaim itself "The Ramona Sentinel" until 1901. The paper, which has been serving the back country since 1887, was first hatched in the thriving mining town of Julian and was called simply "The Sentinel" for the first 14 years it was in business.

That 1928 article credited James A. Jasper as being the first publisher of the Sentinel, but according to an account Jasper himself related in a short unpublished history of Julian, he was actually the second owner of the paper. He later went on to distinguish himself as one of San Diego's better county supervisors.

Seems Jasper was just one of several investors at the very beginning and, well -- why not let him tell it in his own words? From "Julian and Round-About", written in 1928, (and yes, we admit to borrowing part of his title for our book.), we quote:

"I am not cursed with egotism, I crave not vain glory, but when necessity drives, modesty must give the right-of-way to expediency, and hereafter where circumstances compel me to play a part in these memoirs I shall employ the personal pronoun 'I' in defiance of the critic's carp.

"The dawn of 1887 found the people of Julian rioting in new-born courage and ripe for exploitation. New settlers were coming in and building new homes. Orchards, vineyards and gardens were again being planted, new schools were being established, countless cattle roamed the hills, the mining industry had taken on a new lease of life, old shafts were being re-opened, miners were delving into the earth and bringing up golden treasure, and once again stamps were dropping on pay ore.

"Such were the flattering prospects of camp just seventeen years after the discovery of the Washington mine, which lured A.J. Jerkins to camp. He came unheralded, dropped off the stage with a printer's rule and shooting-stick and the startling information that Julian was in sore need of a newspaper, and that he had come with the brains and experience to start it, provided the people would finance the enterprise in the sum of $600. Of course the $600 was a gift, a subsidy for the public benefit.

"A meeting was called, the bait swallowed, hook, line and sinker, the money raised, the plant installed, and on March 14, 1887 the first issue of The Julian Sentinel appeared as a six-column quarto with patent innards

and boiler-plate veneer. The writer put $20 in the pot and drew a bunch of trouble, as will soon appear.

"*The Sentinel plant was parked in the lean-to of Hale & Porters saloon, the only available place in town; the room had but one door, and it opened out onto the main street. On a Sunday evening, shortly after the paper was established, Sam Porter, in cold blood, shot and killed an unarmed Mexican in front of the Sentinal office, and his lifeless body crumpled down in the door where it remained until the justice of the peace (acting coroner) arrived, held an inquest and removed the corpse. Porter put up a plea of self defense, and as there was no effort made to get conflicting evidence, he was exonerated. It was all over in thirty minutes.*

"*At that time I lived three miles out of town, but such news travels fast, and I soon heard of the murder. The Saturday following I went to town, got the Sentinel and scanned its columns, even to the patent inside, for the account of the murder, but no mention of it could I find. I had never been inside a printing office, but I was hot, and with the Sentinal still in my hand I walked in and asked Jenkins who did his reporting. "I do it myself," he replied. "Why do you ask?"*

"*I heard there was a murder in town Sunday, but no one would ever know it by reading the Sentinel," I answered. "Why don't you hire a small boy, perhaps he wouldn't overlook a little thing like murder." "Where were you when this killing was done?"*

"*Me!" he exclaimed. "I was right here in the office and couldn't get out; the man fell right in the office door; don't you see the blood there? It would have been as much as my life is worth to have mentioned the matter, for Hale came in here next morning and told me if I mentioned the killing he would blow up the office and me with it.*

"So that's the way the wind blows is it?" I said. "Well Jenkins, I'll say you are not the man to run a paper in a mining camp like Julian."

"Don't I know it now, "he replied. "If I could only get away I would go today."

"Well," said I, "how much cash will it take to get you on the way?"

"Six hundred dollars and I'll be glad to go." he answered.

"Well" said I, "put that in writing, give me a week's time and if I can find a man in the mountains who can get out a paper, you can go." When I left the office I carried an option on the plant."

As it developed, Jasper was unable to find anyone in the area interested in taking over the paper. He did find a local school teacher, W.A. Sickler, who would take over the editing and management, but only if Jasper rode herd on the finances. He closed the deal with Jenkins, who agreed to stay and set the type and print the paper until Sickler's school was out.

That's how the Sentinel got started and how James A. Jasper broke into the newspaper business. He reported the bad with the good, and after a show-down or two with town bullies, they realized he was one newsman who couldn't be intimidated.

Jasper moved the paper to Nuevo in June 1893, where it continued to carry the same flag it used in Julian i.e.; "The Sentinel", with a logo placed between those two words showing an apple superimposed on a miner's pick and shovel. The town name in the dateline became "Nuevo" and remained so until after the post office name was changed to "Ramona" in June 1895.

Until that time, ads appearing in the paper called the town Nuevo, i.e., "J.A. Verlaque, The Pioneer Merchant of Nuevo", and an ad for a Christmas night party, "Mas-

JAMES A. JASPER, A MAN FOR ALL SEASONS. Shown here playing the role of back country constable, which he had been in earlier days in Julian. Jasper bought the Julian Sentinel shortly after it was started in 1887 and moved it to Nuevo in 1893. He served as County Supervisor 1893 until 1905 when he resigned to become chairman of the San Diego Chamber of Commerce. He was later appointed county emissary, travelling throughout the nation to promote the San Diego area.

querade Dance, at Nuevo Town Hall."

Jasper sold the paper to his assistant editor, Edward C. Foreman, in September 1894 in order to devote more time to his job as a San Diego County supervisor. He was later quoted as saying, "I ran that newspaper nine years, and then gave it away and made a better bargain than when I bought it. Never in the time I owned it did it pay expenses for a single month."

From that time until 1900 it was published in turn by Foreman, Fred J. Perry and Stanley B. Wilson. Wilson also served as the first minister of the Ramona Congregational Church. John G. Overshiner took charge of the Sentinel in February 1900.

EARLY SENTINEL "FLAGS". The "Ramona" Sentinel came into being with the September 19, 1901 edition. While the paper was moved to Nuevo in 1893, it continued to carry the old Julian logo, an apple imposed on a pick and shovel, for eight more years. So far as local businessmen, government records and The Sentinel were concerned, the town was Nuevo until June 1895 when the post office name was changed to Ramona. Note date line on top edition.

It wasn't until the September 19, 1901 edition, that the paper finally dropped the old Julian format for its 'flag' and officially proclaimed itself "The Ramona Sentinel."

In 1902, D.N. Dodson bought the paper from Overshiner, bringing with him a vast background of printing and writing experience.

While running the Ramona Sentinel, Dodson, having been a former justice of the peace in Texas, also filled in as temporary judge of the Ramona Justice Court when Judge Hampton Sloane was either out of town or incapacitated. Sloane, who as a young man had been a journalist in Illinois, was known to reciprocate by helping run the paper when Dodson was under the weather.

Dodson's observations paint a colorful picture of Ramona during the early part of this century, and are found in the chapter of this book covering that period.

From 1908 until 1916, when the paper was acquired by C. A. Seay, the Sentinel was published by L.B. Shook, Henry M. Calkins, A.O. Reed and Timothy Brownhill. Reed later published a paper in La Jolla. Seay controlled it until 1921 when the firm of Smith & Sons bought it. C.O. Smith was editor, and operated the paper until 1931. The Smiths utilized their own special layout for the Sentinel, one column photos, or none at all, no story headline wider than one column, six galleys of print with very few interruptions

In the early days the paper was printed on an old-fashioned Washington hand press, but some time during Reed's regime, a small cylinder press was installed.

During the 1930s, and into the mid-40s the names of Roy Williams, Tex and Lambreth Hancock and Jack Decker were associated with the paper.

The Griffin family, Arthur and Ann, bought the paper in 1946, beginning a long Ramona Sentinel dynasty which lasted over 35 years. Arthur came from a long line of newspaper people. His son, Tom became the sixth generation of newspaper Griffins when he took the reins from his parents.

The Griffins, Tom and wife Carol, sold their interests in 1982 after having built up the paper's circulation to 5,200. The next owner was Walter F. Probst who in turn sold it

THE SENTINEL HAS HAD MANY "FLAG" FORMATS OVER THE YEARS. Shown here is the current one along with a 1958 and a 1914 version. It was about 1958 that Sentinel publisher Tom Griffin started using "In the Valley of the Sun" in the paper's flag. That town slogan has lasted longer than any of the dozens used in the previous 70 years. The Cuymaca News offered some competition around 1909 - 1910 and the edition shown here features Ramona pioneer Hiram Keyes' wedding anniversary.

two years later to the Pomerado Publishing and Printing Company, owned by R. W. "Ward" Calvert. It is published today as part of the Pomerado Newspaper Group, with Duane Spencer, publisher and Maureen Robertson, editor.

The remarkable history of the Ramona Sentinel lies in the number of different owners involved over the past 100-plus years. With the exception of Jasper, Dodson,

Seay, Smith, Williams, Griffin and Pomerado, none of the other 16 owners stayed longer than two years.

Other newspapers have tried their luck here over the years. One was the Cuyamaca News, published in 1909 and 1910 by the husband and wife team of Edwin B. and Katharine A. Tilton. No records have been found to tell us how long this venture lasted. We know by an old letter dated May 10, 1910 from Edwin to John Schwartz, county treasurer and candidate that year for re-election, that Tilton was indeed active and competing with the Sentinel for advertising. "The 'Cuyamaca News', Tilton wrote, "endorses your candidacy for re-election and respectfully solicits the patronage of publishing your announcement. Our paper reaches practically every voter in Ramona, Julian and Mesa Grande Townships, and a little investment in 'printer's ink' would doubtless be judicious."

Edwin got the job that year as United States Census enumerator for those back country townships. This not only provided some extra cash for the Tilton household, no doubt, but also a fine opportunity to sell a few subscriptions and do a bit of campaigning at the same time.

Vol.I, No.I of the paper dated April 28, 1909, spelled out Tilton's editorial policy,"Cuyamaca News editorials are guaranteed to be strictly accurate as well as original. No copying without full credit."

It was not uncommon, however, in those days for the local country newspaper to sell political endorsements, and seemingly in an open fashion. The editor and manager of the Ramona Sentinel in 1914 was Timothy Brownhill. He was a lawyer and former member of the Oregon state legislature. While in Ramona, he helped organize the short lived Chamber of Commerce of North San Diego County.

The 1914 primary election was held on August 25 and the general on Nov. 3. For several weeks before each of those elections, the Sentinel carried articles about the various

TIMOTHY BROWNHILL WAS PUBLISHING THE SENTINEL AROUND 1914. His style was to promote Ramona at every opportunity. He was a former Oregon state legislator and attorney and organized the north San Diego County Chamber of Commerce. His liberal use of photographs was rather progressive for a back country paper in those days.

candidates. Several items were outright endorsements, but the publisher preferred to print them as "news" rather than relegate them to the editorial page. As the election date neared, the volume of campaign ads steadily grew in the weekly Friday editions, until Oct. 30 when nearly one third of the Sentinel's eight pages were filled with ads for congressional and state legislative candidates, as well as for the offices of sheriff, district attorney, coroner, etc.

On Nov. 6, Brownhill's paper came out as usual on Friday. But not one word was found in its pages about the results of that preceding Tuesday election. Nor was there anything about it in the following Friday edition. There were the usual reports about town happenings, and the weekly episode from Rex Beach's novel, "Ne'er Do Well, A Romance of the Panama Canal". But, so far as the Sentinel was concerned, it was as though the election had been called off and the paper had simply forgotten to let anyone know about it.

Apparently, the responsibility for reporting election results in those days was left to the metropolitan papers such as the San Diego Union. The local paper's charge, it appears, was to provide a forum (for pay) for the county-wide candidates, and that being done, the country press went back to its mainly local news coverage; such items as the Ramona Women's Club activities, church news and chit chat about who was visiting whom from such and such a place.

The newspaper business, like most businesses, attracts competition and there have been several times over the years when the Ramona market seemed a bright opportunity for a new venture.

One such paper was the Ramona News which was published in 1983. The News was a weekly and was distributing 8,000 free copies to all Ramona households. While the paper was able to attract some substantial advertisers, according to David Ross, former managing editor, publication was suspended after eight months. Its publisher was Joe Booth, Jr.

Another local paper is the San Vicente Valley News which is published monthly and celebrated its first anniversary in March 1989. Its primary audience are the owners of property within the covenant area of the planned community of San Diego Country Estates. It has a circulation of 3,400, features mainly events and happenings within that valley and is published by the community property owner's association. The Valley News' managing editor is Laura Brien.

13

Law & Order

A judiciary era came to an end in 1976 when the Ramona Justice court was put out of business by a new state law. For over eighty-five years Ramona had its own court and judge, but the new law required all counties with municipal court systems to take over justice courts and incorporate them into their municipal system. Thus it was that Ramona became a branch of the El Cajon Municipal Court, and judges other than those who were locally elected took over the job of adjudicating local cases.

The first justice court in the Santa Maria Valley was founded in 1890 and named the Nuevo Township court. Up until that time, back country cases involving Santa Maria Valley matters were handled by the Ballena justice of the peace, or in the City of San Diego.

In 1902 the name was changed to the Santa Maria Township court but that lasted only seven months until it was again changed, this time to the Ramona Court.

The last man to be elected Ramona justice of the peace was retired Navy Commander Will L. Stalnaker, who held the position from 1965 to 1975. Under the old system, a justice court judge was not required to be a lawyer. The only qualification necessary was the trust his fellow citizens had in his abilities, common sense and honesty, as shown at the polls on election day. Judge Stalnaker later went on to get his law degree, pass the State bar and establish a private legal practice.

One of the earliest judges to preside over a Santa Maria Valley justice court was retired Civil War Captain, Hampton P. Sloane, who held the office from 1901 to 1906. He was the only one to have had any previous judicial experience when he took office. As a young man he had been assistant editor of the Rockport (Illinois) Register and played a prominent role in starting the first county agricultural society in the State of Illinois. With the outbreak of civil war, Sloane helped organize Company C of the Illinois Volunteer Infantry and was chosen Captain. He fought in the battles of Perryville and Stone River.

After the war, he moved to Johnson County Missouri where he was appointed justice of the peace in 1868 and became a controversial figure there when he gave the right to vote to 60 Confederate veterans. His colorful post-war career also included a stint at operating a stage line carrying the U. S. Mail, and reporting and editing for a Missouri newspaper. He left the mid-west for California in 1890 settling in the Sweetwater Valley for five years before purchasing a ranch in Ramona.

Occasionally, when Sloane was incapacitated or out of town, D. N. Dodson filled in as pro-tem judge. Dodson was editor and proprietor of the Ramona Sentinel and sometimes signed his name with the letters "J. P.", followed parenthetically with the note "(Which means Jackass of the Peace)". However, Dodson had as much, or more experience with the law as any. He was a member of the Texas bar, had served as mayor of Denton Texas as well as having been a justice of the peace there as well.

The man who was Ramona's judge the longest period of time, 1906 until 1949, was James F. Kelly, a native of Ohio and a farmer. He came to Ramona in 1903 at age 32, suffering from acute asthma and looking for a climate more beneficial to his health. Kelly first lived in a tent behind the Old Adams House, but the conditions suited him just fine, and weather proved to be what he needed.

Not long after he arrived he became aware of a feud between two prominent ranchers who were on the brink of a shoot-out. The long-standing animosity had made the situation in Ramona rather unpleasant, and the town was having a problem getting anyone to stay as justice of the peace. Strolling into Jack Bachelder's harness shop one sunny afternoon, the tall, lanky newcomer named Kelly commented on the situation. "Well, I'd like to be judge around here just long enough to call their bluff," he drawled, whacking at a stick with his knife.

A petition was quickly circulated and the County Board Of Supervisors named him justice of the peace.

Calling in one of the gun-toting ranchers, Judge Kelly said; "You've been causing a lot of trouble around these parts, threatening to shoot your neighbor. Now I don't think you're as tough as you think you are, so I'm going to put you under a $500 peace bond, and the next time you start anything, it'll mean about six months in jail for you." That ended the feud.

While presiding over the Ramona Justice Court for those many years, Kelly substituted on the San Diego bench as well. He also sat as pro-tem police judge in the city for eight years during the late 1920s and early 1930s.

He had a deep interest in the youth of Ramona and served on the school district board of trustees. Many a teenager who was brought up before Judge Kelly on traffic and other offenses long remembers him as a stern, but most

JUDGE H.P. SLOANE WAS A CIVIL WAR VETERAN HAVING COM-MANDED AN ILLINOIS INFANTRY COMPANY. Sloane was the first Ramona justice of the peace who had any previous judicial experience. He was also a journalist who filled in for Sentinel editor D.N. Dodson when needed. In turn Dodson, who had been a J.P. in Texas, would fill in.on the bench for Sloane.

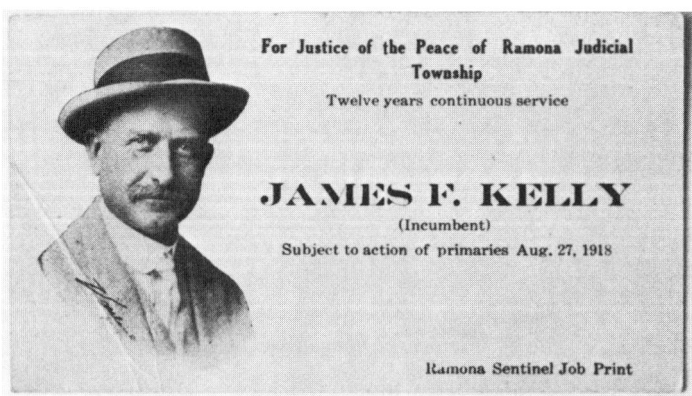

JUDGE JAMES F. KELLY HELD THE JOB OF RAMONA J.P. LONGER THAN ANY OTHER. He served from 1906 until 1949. Kelly was also active on the school board of trustees for many years. Campaign card is for his 1918 re-election campaign.

understanding and humane person. Kelly's 43 years on the Ramona bench stands as a county record for longevity as a justice of the peace.

From 1949 until 1963, former trucking operator A.C. Bisher served as justice. A.P. Holly, real estate broker and turkey rancher was elected to the office when Bisher retired.

Holly was the only Ramona J.P. to be called 'Judge' before he ever sat on a court bench. Seems he was founder of Ramona's annual Turkey Day celebrations. For 25 years had also traveled all over the U.S. judging at turkey shows. He died in 1964 having served only six months of his elected term as a Ramona justice of the peace.

With the office of justice of the peace being eliminated shortly after Stalnacker's retirement in 1975, two judges served briefly in the court's closing days. They were Alfred H. Dart and Gerald Lewis.

Back Country Constables

Early day constables in the Ramona area had to furnish their own transportation and guns. If they were tracking a horse thief or cattle rustler, they went about their business on horseback. Otherwise they used a spring wagon. They carried a bedroll, coffee pot and a pan or two to do some cooking, since their missions often would keep them away from home overnight.

The last of the real old-time constables, John Stevens, went about his business in a similar manner right up until 1956 when he retired from the County Sheriff's Department. The only difference was, instead of the spring wagon, John drove a vintage Buick touring sedan. But he still went out on horseback, when that was what it took to get the job done.

Stevens was a genuine cowboy from New Mexico. He came to San Diego County in 1923 and herded cattle for

George Sawday and Oliver Sexton on the Los Penasquitos
Rancho. Sexton was chief deputy under County Sheriff
James Byers and recommended Stevens for appointment
to fill a vacancy in the office in 1927. Among other assign-
ments, Stevens worked the Mexican border during prohibition. His background as a cowboy came into good use in
tracking and dealing with the cattle rustlers who occasionally practiced their evil work in the back country.

But with the election of 1934 and a new regime in the
sheriff's office, almost all the deputies were replaced by
the new sheriff's own men. These were the days before civil
service, and Stevens went back to herding cattle. In 1936,
however, he was reinstated when the new civil service
system was established. He was assigned to Ramona and
was responsible for a territory ranging north to the Riverside County line and east to Imperial county. He and
deputy August Grand of Julian worked closely in covering
this vast area and became close friends.

During the 20 years Stevens was Ramona deputy, he had
a special relationship with the youth of the community. He
knew where they were and they knew he knew! He sometimes would be waiting for them when they arrived home
after some misdeed and would have a good talk with them.
When talk failed, which it rarely did, Stevens employed
sterner methods.

An announcement was placed in the Ramona Sentinel
classified section during the late 1940s that read, "TO
THAT: Foreign born gent that stole my pick plow. If you
don't get it back pronto you will receive a call from Johnny
Stevens. (Signed) Fred Creelman."

Stevens' wife Lois, who also served in the justice system
in Ramona as clerk of the court, recalled recently that once
there was a complaint filed with headquarters that Stevens
was running around on personal matters while driving a
county car. "The facts were, John had no county car. He was

JOHN STEVENS WAS RAMONA'S LAST "OLD TIME CONSTABLE".
Shown here in formal deputy sheriff uniform in the 1950s, John was
more comfortable in boots and Levis when tracking down cattle
rustlers.

WIFRED E. WOODWARD LATER BECAME ONE OF THE TOWN'S MORE
SUCCESSFUL BUSINESSMEN. However, in earlier years he put in his
share of time keeping the peace in the back country. Woodward
was Ramona constable 1901 to 1907.

on call seven days a week and 24 hours a day, and had to furnish his own car."

Ramona lawmen during the era around the turn of the century included W.W. Minor who was appointed constable in 1890. He was followed soon after by C.S. Sloane who served until 1895 when rancher J.W. Haworth of San Vicente Valley took over for the next six years.

In 1901, W.E. Woodward, a dairy farmer and real estate broker, was constable and performed the duties until 1907. About this time, the Ramona Tent Village was a popular attraction for folks who wanted to get away and spend time under the spreading oak trees. People from all over the county came to this Goose Valley resort to enjoy its many activities.

Moonshiners knew however, according to Arthur Woodward, that there was a ready market for their fire-water and sold their wares at these gatherings. Problems would result for the peace seeking family clientele when a few of the locals, including Indians, drank too much. Constable Woodward was known to tie some of the more obstreperous imbibers in a sitting position with their arms around the trees. But their compadres would slip up on them, tip their heads back and pour what they could down their throats. When the constable made his rounds to release the offenders, he found them drunker than when he tied them up. After the first few times, the tree tying method was abandoned and recalcitrants hauled off to the 8x10 iron town jail.

"Hosey" Van Loon assumed the office of constable when W.E. Woodward retired in 1907, but he didn't last long. According to Arthur Woodward, he was known for being a nitpicker when it came to non-violent infractions of the law. At night, he took pleasure in stopping all horse-drawn vehicles which did not have a white light that could be seen from the front and back.

It seems that on one dark night, a six-horse team was hauling quite a load heading east in the 700 block of Main Street. Hosey gruffly hollered, "Stop in the name of the law", and asked the driver where his lights were.

"No savvy, no speak English," replied LaChappa of Mesa Grande. Hosey lit a match, went to the rear of the wagon and said, "See, you have to have a light back here." This continued for about 20 minutes with much encouragement from the bystanders.

Finally, LaChappa stated in a very clear voice, "Mr. Constable, if you set this load on fire by your demonstrations, you and Ramona will be blown to hell and gone. This is a load of dynamite I am taking to the mines in Mesa Grande." At that, La Chappa released the brakes and with a giddyup was on his way. Hosey was the laughing stock of the locals and this ended his career as a constable.

14

Vibrant 20s

The little town of Ramona experienced a banner decade during the 1920s. Population stood only at about 700 to 750. But there was a vibrancy about the community. Things were getting done and the town was on the move. "It was an exciting time," recalls Cynthia Kunkel, who as a small girl was impressed by "the many new projects and progress being made, especially around 1925 and 1926."

Electricity came to Ramona. Main Street was paved. A water district was formed. School districts were being unified. The Masons built a grand new hall at the corner of Main and Eighth. The first concrete formed building took shape, (today we call it the Turkey Inn). The first state franchised truck route between Ramona and San Diego was established.

The fragmented school system, which saw four different school districts doing business in the Ramona area, began unification about this time. The Santa Maria district was merged with the Ramona district in May 1921, and the Earl District voted to join the Union District in June 1925. It

1925- TOP ROW L-R, PROF. JOHN WILSON, JACK SIMS, HARRY BARNES, CLARENCE SMITH, GEORGE TELFORD. FRONT ROW R-L, GUY WOODWARD, BOB STEPHENS, JOHN NIXON.

"PROF" WILSON AND ONE OF HIS MANY CHAMPIONSHIP BASKET-BALL TEAMS. Coach Wilson was also high school principal, teacher and district superintendent. Total number of students in the Ramona high school then was 35, yet Wilson's teams were able to beat the big city schools. Coach and students shown in front of "Prof's" Essex, which also served as the team bus.

was two decades later in 1943, however, that elementary school unification was completed when the Spring Hill District voted to become part of the Ramona Union Grammar School District.

In 1917 a young man of 32, with a remarkable background in teaching and coaching, moved to Ramona to assume the duties of principal and teacher at the high school. He stayed for the rest of the 50 years that he lived, continually active in furthering academic excellence in Ramona. His name was John H. Wilson, but he was affectionately known as "Prof" Wilson by his many students and friends. "Prof" had taught languages at Texas Christian University and Alhambra High School. He then spent six years teaching and coaching at Whittier High School where his basketball teams won four consecutive state championships.

RAMONA HIGH SCHOOL BOARD OF TRUSTEES 1920. Sitting is Olive Peirce and Thomas Reynolds. Standing; Bruce Dye, James Dukes and James Kelly. In recent years, a new elementary school in San Vicente Valley was named for James Dukes, and the new junior high school after Olive Pierce.

RAMONA'S FIRST PERMANENT HIGH SCHOOL, Built in 1912 and torn down in 1935, "The Old Cement Building" housed a total student body of but 30 to 40 during the 1920s. The up-stairs had two classrooms and an auditorium, down-stairs was the typing room, girls' cooking room and the boys' shop. Painting is by Louise Shidner.

Wilson was hired by a school board consisting of James Dukes, Olive Peirce, Bruce Dye, Judge Kelly and Thomas Reynolds. In later years, the pioneer Bruce Dye would remark that the hiring of "Prof" was the single best thing they did for Ramona.

Ramona High School had a grand total of 30 in its student body in 1921. Staff, including principal numbered five. But even with such a small enrollment, the school offered a full high school curriculum. Four levels of history were taught, and required. Basketball was the only sport in which Ramona was able to field a league team, but what a team they had that year! With a total student body consisting of only 12 to 14 boys, Coach 'Point a Minute' Wilson was able to assemble a five man team that beat all the big county schools, including San Diego and Grossmont and went on to the Southern California finals in Long Beach. When Ramona High was playing basketball, there was many a local business that closed early so the proprietor could "go down the hill" to see the game.

In 1936, when the first high school complex was built, (the buildings which now house the school district headquarters, and are named in Wilson's honor), "Prof" gave up his coaching duties to become the first superintendent of the Ramona Unified School District. He continued, however, to serve also as principal and teacher until retiring in 1947. Even after retirement, he never left teaching and learning. He tutored students for the rest of his life as well as translating several foreign languages and teaching himself new ones.

As the new year 1922 dawned, the Ramona Improvement Society was renamed the Ramona Chamber of Commerce with a rededication to further the town's promising potential. John Bargar was president that year. It was the C of C, in those days, that was ever on the alert and provided leadership in all matters affecting the community's physical well being.

By 1924, there was so much community spirit, in fact, that Ramona boosters were actually using four slogans and the C of C had to run a contest to see which one to settle on. The winner was "The Golden Valley of Little Ranches". Other slogans having been promoted, but henceforth declared unofficial, were "A Paradise for Poultry", The Heart of San Diego County" and "The Valley of Ranches, Riches, Romance and Indian Lore".

As it developed, that winning slogan lasted less than five years. The chamber's stationary in the 1929 proclaimed Ramona as "The Heart of San Diego County", and by the 1940s the chamber's slogan was "Heart of the Heaven on Earth Country, Above the Fog Line, Below the Snow Line."

In 1958, Tom Griffin, who was running the Sentinel, decided to tag the town in the newspaper's flag as, "In the Valley of the Sun". The folks liked that so well, that now after 30 years the slogan still seems to be accepted as official by all Ramona factions.

The earliest town slogan the writer has been able to find was used by the Sentinel in 1904. Their flag proclaimed Ramona as being, "At the Gateway of the Mountain Country."

The community spirit of the 1920s manifested itself not only in town boosterism and physical improvements, but in citizenship as well. The California Development Association sponsored a contest, starting in 1924, to encourage greater voter registration throughout the State. A $100 silver citizenship cup was offered as a prize to any community with a chamber of commerce that could get the highest percentage of registered voters to the polls in the general elections.

Much enthusiasm was generated throughout the state. Many towns and cities, large and small, took up the challenge for the honor and Ramona went all out. On election

THE COMMUNITY OF RAMONA EARNED THE RIGHT TO KEEP THIS SIL-VER CITIZENSHIP CUP for the best voter turnout in California, four general elections in a row.

day in 1924 leaders rounded up voters and drove them to town. Students were excused from school early to help check the polls and make phone calls. When the tally was finished, Ramona had turned out 318 of their 339 registered voters for the statewide winning percentage of 93.8%.

The contest provided that a community could permanently retain the Silver Cup if it won three successive times. In 1926 Ramona voters responded with a 98.33% turnout, 354 voting of the total 360 registered. Of the six who failed to vote that year, three were gravely ill, two were out of town on business and the sixth, the fire warden, away fighting a forest fire. Ramona won the contest for a third time, and the honor of permanently retaining the cup in 1928 with a 98.64%. Good citizenship had developed into a habit when the town put in another winning performance with their 97.8% turnout for good measure in 1930.

The big flood of 1916 had washed out the San Diego Cuyamaca and Eastern's tracks between Foster and Lakeside, and by 1922 more track was missing between

CREELMAN'S OLD BLACKSMITH SHOP CONVERTED TO TAKE CARE OF THE HORSELESS CARRIAGE. L.P. Codington's garage and gas station in 1924 (where Sal's Plumbing stands today). Not only could you get your auto serviced, but also a shave and a haircut.

there and Santee. The track that was lost in those floods was never replaced. People of the back country, however, were beginning to depend less upon the railroad and more upon motor vehicles. The train to Foster soon went out of business. With the railroad's eastern terminus moving further west and county roads steadily improving, haulers of freight were by-passing the railroad more and more.

A.C. Bisher, known as Bert and later as Judge, was a new arrival from Canada. He recognized a need for direct shipments into San Diego to save the double handling of freight at the railhead. By 1922 he had established a successful freight business and his company was the first to receive a state franchise for hauling between San Diego and at the railhead. By 1922 he had established a successful freight business and his company was the first to receive a state franchise for hauling between San Diego and Ramona that year. The Bisher Trucking Company is still serving the town today.

WINTERS' BAKERY ON THE CORNER OF 6TH AND MAIN. Joe Winters stands in front of the new building in 1926. The building, looking much as it did then, has more recently housed a real estate office. Unfortunately it burned to the ground this spring, 1989.

In 1924, electricity finally reached the Santa Maria Valley. Lights and power were made available with a connection at the San Pasqual terminal. The Ramona Lighting District was formed that year and local taxpayers were assessed on their county tax bills the $35,000 total it cost to extend the lines.

On Jan. 22, 1924, the San Diego Union reported that the county board of supervisors instructed their highway engineer to prepare plans and specifications for a stretch of pavement six miles in length to run through Ramona Valley. It was to start at the eastern edge of town and run westerly to a point near the head of Mussey Grade Highway.

In December 1924, the Sentinel noted that Ramona, not being an incorporated city, had no official records on building permits. However, they estimated there had been "no less than 20 new houses and seven new business buildings erected, besides fully as many garages, barns, chicken houses, etc., and probably more than that number of wells dug."

Ramona's Castle

In 1916, an imposing castle began taking shape on the northern slope of Mount Woodson. It was to be the dream home of Irene Amy Strong who purchased the Woodson Ranch seven years earlier.

The mansion stands today, much as it was when finished in 1921, having been well cared for over these many years. The estate is presently owned by a development firm, which plans to preserve its character and charm, utilizing it as a clubhouse and focal point for a new golf course and planned residential community.

Amy Strong was not merely a seamstress or dressmaker, as she was listed in the San Diego directory, but a highly successful couturiere, having among her clients Madam Ernestine Schuman-Heink, the Babcocks and other members of the San Diego and Coronado social elite.

IRENE AMY STRONG SUPERVISED THE BUILDING OF THIS MANSION FROM 1916 UNTIL 1921. It stands at the northern foot of Mount Woodson, looking very much today as it did when finished nearly 70 years ago. "The Castle" as it is called, will serve as the clubhouse for a new residential and golf community currently being built on the old Strong ranch.

She hired the design firm of Weaver and Vawter to carry out her concept of avant garde architecture. The end product was a multi-level, 27 room, 12,000 square foot home with four to eight foot thick walls. Building materials of the main house included eucalyptus logs for ceiling beams, oak, redwood, native rocks picked from the slopes of Mount Woodson, flagstone, adobe, bricks and tile, plaster, concrete and stucco.

Since trained craftsmen were unable to adjust to her unconventional approach to building, she had to settle for a building crew made up of local laborers. No chalk lines were used in the construction. There are no perfect corners and neither the roof nor floors are level.

The net result, however, has been described by many as majestic and charming; a unique estate whose design has worn well over the years.

The State Bank of Ramona was running ads in 1927, boasting

"Paid up capital of $32,500." Safety deposit boxes were available for rent, and the bank paid 4% interest on savings accounts. Officers were, S. Rotanzi, president; R.L. Jerman, 1st vice president; and George Sawday, 2nd vice president.

Item in the 3/2/28 Sentinel:

"Rollin Peirce commences duties as local editor of the Sentinel. He will be found at the old stand in the C of C building, telephone Ramona 16. Mr. Peirce also has been made secretary of the C of C and the Ramona Irrigation District, the positions having been held by Miss Elizabeth Seay for several years. The change is the result of Miss Seay's resignation."

15

Water

Southern California's history essentially revolves around water development. Ramona's is no different. Those towns that succeeded in meeting their growing water needs were the towns that flourished. Those that failed, either aren't around today, or never grew past their first few water wells.

Today, in 1989, Ramona is served by a modern metropolitan water district covering over 75 square miles and with an assessed valuation in excess of $890 million. The District contains 46,939 acres, of which about 17,000 acres are served with appoximately 10,000 acre feet of water annually through 7,067 domestic and agricultural water meters. But it was not until the mid-1920s that Ramona even had a community water service, and the mid-1950s until the current broad-based district was formed.

Water development in Ramona started with early efforts at enlarging springs and impounding their meager flows along with the runoff from occasional storms. Digging wells followed. Those methods sufficed to a degree, but barely kept pace with growing essential needs. The farmer, who was the average Ramonan, was a captive of fickle weather cycles. When the inevitable drought years came, so came hardship and often ruin.

Around the turn of the century, Ramona even had its own flume. It was a one-foot by one-foot open redwood chute, according to Guy Woodward, and ran about three miles, from Hatfield Creek to 10th Street, just east of the present alignment of San Vicente Road. The flume, which shows on an early Santa Maria Land and Water Company map was built by that company about 1888. Water was impounded in a 50-x25-x8-foot reservoir on the Thomas Converse farm. Apparently the system proved to be more work than it was worth because it was later dismantled and the lumber salvaged by Luther Janeway to build a new home.

JohnMykrantz had no sooner purchased most of the San Vicente Valley from the Morettis in 1922, than he set out on an ambitious plan to harness the valley's watershed with a series of dams. While the project helped the local job market and boosted the Ramona economy, it proved a riparian failure. The City of San Diego challenged his right to impound as much water as his main dam could hold. And while he was able to establish some water rights, he was forced to lower the dam. The great flood of 1926, however, made the whole fight academic. All of his check dams and the main dam either silted up or washed out.

First Water District

By the early 1920s Ramona's population stood at about 725. Practically every house in and near the town center had a water well, but unfortunately each also had a cesspool or septic system. As the water table receded each year, and cesspools were reaching the water level, it was becoming apparent something had to be done.

Ramona has been fortunate to have had a few leaders with vision and the ability to get things done. Standing tall among them was John C. Barger, the father of Ramona's community water system.

In a "Recompilation" written by Barger in 1938, he told of how the Ramona Irrigation District got its start. Mrs. James Stockton came to him, he wrote, about 1923 and suggested he try to do something about a safe water supply for the town.

Barger had a reputation for being a doer, and an honest one at that. He moved to Ramona as a young man in 1891, when the town was still called Nuevo. Barger came from the same town in Missouri as the George Telford family. He was hired to help tend the Telford's live stock when the family moved west by rail box car. Barger also helped the Telfords build their new home, and liked Nuevo so well, he decided to stay. Four years later, he and Telford's youngest daughter, Ida were married. He later became the area's leading plumber and mechanic, as well as hardware store and lumberyard owner and eventually was responsible for installing over 300 windmills in the back country. He also helped organize and build the first telephone line linking the back country with San Diego. So when the town needed something done, it was only natural that people would look to Barger for help.

"I promised her (Mrs. Stockton) that as soon as I could spare the time I would go to San Diego and see Ed Fletcher," wrote Barger, "for if there was anyone who would and could help, it was Ed." It seemed to many in those days that Fletcher was involved in just about every water development plan or project in San Diego County since the Padres dammed Mission Gorge.

Barger drove down to San Diego and saw Fletcher who agreed to come up to Ramona and take a look at the

JOHN BARGAR, A DOMINANT LEADER DURING THE FIRST HALF OF
THE 20TH CENTURY. Bargar was the father of Ramona's first community water system as well as its fire department and telephone
system. A man who was always in the forefront.

possibilities. Bargar's plan was to pump water from
Stockton's 68 acres to a tank on a hill just east of the Santa
Maria Creek plain.

About this time, Ramona Chamber of Commerce
leaders, concerned with the impending water problem
were also scheduling meetings to see what could be done.

Fletcher drove up to Ramona as promised one Sunday
morning to go over Bargar's plan. The two were standing
on the proposed site for a storage tank, viewing the situation, (across from the present water district's office on
Earlham Avenue) when, according to Bargar, Fletcher
asked,

"What is all that green down there?", Fletcher was looking at the Santa Maria Creek flood plain where the
Ramona Community Park is now located.

"Its Mr. Woodward's corn and alfalfa." Bargar answered.

"Where does he get all his water?" Fletcher asked.

"From the pumping plant at the foot of this hill." replied
Barger.

"Then" said Fletcher, "buy all that land clear down to the
bridge."

"My God, Fletcher," Bargar exclaimed, "that will cost too much."

Fletcher was emphatic,"Ramona can't afford not to do it."

As was usually the case when it came to matters concerning water resources, Ed Fletcher was right. All that well field area, and then some, later proved vitally essential to meet the town's future demands.

The land was owned by W. E. Woodward, local real estate broker and town leader who ran one of the more successful farm operations in Ramona. Much of his farm's success came from its location. The Woodwards had drilled 3 shallow wells in the water rich sands of the creek and built a pumping system which produced 1,000 gallons per minute. They irrigated their crops and grazing land from this system. Guy Woodward lived with his uncle and recalls that as a young boy, he would help get the pump going by climbing up on the big fly-wheel of the 15 horsepower Fairbanks-Morse engine and ride it down. "It would usually kick over on the first try with a loud 'phoom'," added Guy.

Woodward had done something else that proved invaluable for Ramona's future. In 1912 he filed for and obtained water rights to 1,000 miner's-inches of waters from the Santa Maria Creek. When the fledgling Ramona Irrigation District (RID) eventually purchased Woodwards' land and wells, they also acquired those valuable water rights.

The County of San Diego also had three wells nearby for pumping water into their Collier Park swimming pool and filling two small tanks, one at the park and one at the Women's Club House.

But forming the district took time, and considerable spirited debate. The Ramona Chamber of Commerce was in the forefront as was the case with most public improvement programs in those days. Ransom Ried, R. L. Jerman and George Comings formed the Chamber water committee with Barger. Many public meetings were held to gain support from the citizens. San Diego County's Congressman Phil Swing came to lend his support. It was Swing and U.S. Senator Hiram Johnson who later teamed up, in 1928, to successfully maneuver the Boulder Dam bill through Congress.

Questions were raised as to the new district's size. Was the plan too small? Should it be larger in order to anticipate future growth? Some argued that yes, taking care of the immediate demand was a vital first phase, but plans should also be made for long term needs.

Ed Fletcher offered strong advice for those who had their reservations about going into debt for the system. If necessary, he himself, he said, would purchase the lands along the creek, and build the necessary improvements. In a letter addressed to E. M. Schlink, chamber president in September 1924, Fletcher stated, "In my opinion it will be an almost criminal act if the businessmen of your community do not take some immediate action of some kind that will protect the future water supply of the town of Ramona. Otherwise some enterprising real estate men in time may lay out a new subdivision, install curbs, sidewalks and street paving, file on the water of the Santa Maria creek, install a water supply, and you will wake up someday to find that the present town of Ramona has real competition. This has been done in other places." and Fletcher added, "There is room for one good town in that valley and the quicker your community wakes up to its possibilities, the better for you all." Fletcher was instrumental in starting the communities of Solana Beach, Fletcher Hills and Rancho Santa Fe, among others, and knew what he was talking about. His son Charles later went on to start Home Federal Savings and Loan in the early 1930s.

The RID was officially formed under the California Irrigation District Act on July 27, 1925, for the principal purpose of providing a domestic water supply to the townsite area consisting of 660 acres.

In a letter appearing in the Ramona Sentinel, August 7, 1925, Mrs Paul D. Ransom wrote, "Came the great news: 'Eighty votes for and only four votes against.' A water district for Ramona! And so at last comes not only a victory for progression, but also a grand fruition for the faithful few who by their unstinted efforts and faithful unselfishness have made possible this great forward step in municipal development. I say 'municipal', for that will be the next logical step in Ramona's advancement."

In May 1926, the citizens again overwhelming supported the district, this time by a vote of 96 to two authorizing the sale of bonds in the amount of $91,000 to finance the purchase of the water-bearing lands, dig a sump and more wells and build a storage and distribution system.

During all this, the Chamber was relying on T.H. King, San Diego civil engineer and water authority, for professional advice. It was his report on the development of the proposed district that served to support the bonding program. King later became the new District's engineer.

Barger was fully immersed in all the trials and tribulations of assuring that an economical system was designed, getting State approvals and putting a bond program together. Water was first delivered through the system in August 1927.

When the first board of directors was selected, Barger was elected to the three member panel along with Clara Keyes Graham and R. L. Jerman. "Lem" Jerman ran the drug store that his father had started in the 1880s.

Clara Keyes Graham

Clara Keyes Graham was the daughter of Ramona pioneer and Civil War veteran, Hiram Keyes. But long before Clara had assumed a leadership role in Ramona water development, she had distingished herself in the teaching field. She had been one of the early one-room school teachers in the area, teaching in the Earle, Ramona and San Pasqual districts from 1892 to 1896. She went on to U.C. Berkeley afterward and was offered a job to teach in the Philippines upon graduation. She worked there for 18 years. While teaching in Manila, one of her students was future U.S. Senator Robert Taft, son of President William Howard Taft who was then governor of the islands. Clara wrote the Philippine supplement to Hunter's Biology in 1912 and arranged a laboratory manual that was used in public schools there for many years. Upon returning to Ramona, Clara became a poultry farmer, and was an early president of the Ramona Poultry Association.

Early Board Meetings

Those early RID boards operated frugally, as Harold Stephen recalls. "Most of the board meetings were held at the 'Geedunk Stand', (slang for soda fountain where Harold worked while going to high school) in Jerman's drug and paint store. Jerman the pharmacist occasionally had to excuse himself from the discussion to fill a prescription." There was no $100 per director for each meeting in those days. The meetings were public in the sense that if anyone was interested in district business, they simply came to the soda fountain and pulled up a chair. Judge James Kelly, Bob Ransom, the town constable and the banker, among others, would often be seen joining in the deliberations. "And the discussions were not confined simply to the subject of water operations." Stephen added, "All the usual things like trying to get the County government to work on our roads and other problems, got a lot of attention at these meeting."

By 1936, the town of Ramona had grown to about 900 and the RID was serving 164 water meters, and pumping over 140 acre feet of water per year.

During the early 1940s it became apparent that a countywide shortage of water was imminent. San Diego was a major center of WWII effort, and a lack of water could prove disastrous. Colorado River water became available as a result of the completion of the Hoover (Boulder) Dam. When the City of San Diego filed for Colorado River water in the early 1930s, some farseeing, unsung city official had fortunately included the County of San Diego in the application as well. This enabled the entire county to join in a San Diego water authority, which was formed in 1944. The San Diego County Water Authority (CWA) became a part of the Southern California Metropolitan Water District (MWD), thus eligible for this new source of imported water.

The Ramona Irrigation District became one of its first members, but joining was not without controversy. One of those who advocated the expansion of the RID, and joining the CWA was Stanley M. Ransom who wrote a letter in the April 7, 1944 edition of the Ramona Sentinel. He urged a "Yes" vote from the voters, because as he said, "We just could not face the future and be honest with our friends and customers with any other attitude. And to the many property owners outside the district who want to see this county progress, and particularly the young men who are coming back from the war to make the Santa Maria Valley their home; I would not care to say that I did not vote to make their future brighter and their chances better."

Writing in opposition, in the same edition, was RID Director Clara Keyes Graham who questioned the costs and benefits of such a move.

The people voted to join, and the RID became one of the original nine member agencies when the CWA was formed in 1944. But Ramona didn't stay long. When in November 1946, San Diego County voters approved a $2 million bond issue to construct aqueduct extensions to the various member districts, the City of Coronado and the Ramona Irrigation District decided to get out of the authority. Coronado because city fathers felt they had enough water resources, and Ramona because RID directors feared excessive costs in lifting the water to the Santa Maria valley. During the 1945-46 season, the RID pumped 306 acre feet of water, an increase of 111 percent from 10 years earlier. But the District was fast depleting its well field water table and when the drought of 1946-47 came, pumping had to be cut back to 234 acre feet that year. Population in Ramona was 1,500 and the RID had 366 water services. The turkey industry was the most important agricultural pursuit. Irrigated acreage served by the RID accounted for a mere 36 acres total, i.e.; citrus 21, deciduous fruits 9, vineyards 2, and pastureland 4.

Water again became the central issue in town in 1948 as it had been in 1925. The drought was limiting the RID's well field recharge and the town was straining to grow. The chamber of commerce again appointed a special water committee in January and requested a joint meeting with the district's board. Pressure was building to find new sources of water. The RID had, only 13 months earlier, burned its bridges when it pulled out of the county water authority. As far as the RID board was concerned, the new source would have to come from somewhere other than the Colorado River.

The district hired a consultant who identified two potential dam sites. One was on the Hatfield Creek three miles east of town, but a dam at that site would only impair the recharge of the district's existing well field. The second site was on the Santa Maria Creek west of town at the lower end of the valley. Problems there were that the City of San Diego owned those water rights. Besides, the district would have to pump the water back up to town, and pumping was what they were attempting to avoid when they dropped out of the authority. The only solution seemed to be the county aquaduct, but RID directors didn't want to bite that bullet.

Wells were running dry again in 1952 and after an eight year impass with the RID, several concerned citizens along with farmers outside the "favored 660 acre" towncenter started to promote formation of a new municipal water district. The new district would serve a much broader, and fast growing Ramona. Forrest Holly, Doc Soister, Bob Till, Tom Griffin and Frank Kunkel were among those in the forefront in this effort.

After two elections, voters in Ramona finally approved the formation of the Ramona Municipal Water District (RMWD) in 1956, and authorized $2 million in water bonds in 1957. The initial district boundaries included 20,600 acres, of which 17,000 was suitable for farming and development. Population within district territory was estimated at 4,400 and assessed valuation was $4.3 million. The first members of the RMWD board of directors were James Smith, H.H. Carter, Everett Romine, Carl Nelson and Neil Stonehouse. First meetings were conducted at the Ramona Women's Club, but later moved to the high school.

Now that Ramona would have an outside supply of water to augment its wells and broaden its service, the question arose: why two water districts when one could do the job better and cheaper? The directors of the two water districts met several times to explore a merger, but it took a vote of the people in February 1957 to settle the issue.

The RID was dissolved and its operations and equipment taken over by the RMWD. The RID had done a fine job for over 30 years. It had provided good service at reasonable rates and never missed a payment to its bond holders, but Ramona had simply outgrown it. The last citizens to serve on that district's board of directors were Oliver Garrett, William Hanigan, Frank Kunkel, Ray

RAMONA HOOKS UP WITH THE CWA. The town was only able to grow past its 660 acre towncenter after it built a line from the aqueduct. Ground breaking ceremonies took place January 1958. Front Row: Doc Soister, Robert Till, County Supervisor Dean Howell, CWA President Fred Heilborn, RMWD directors James Smith, Carl Nelson and Sid Carter. Top Row: RID director Frank Kunkel, Sentinel Editor Donna Warren, RMWD directors Everett Romaine and Jack Kinzer.

West and Richard Thuneman.

Dedication ceremonies were held in July 1958 for the new water system which would bring imported water to Ramona. By 1976, annexations had increased the RMWD's territory to over 46,000 acres, where it has remained constant since. During the later part of the 1970s, the prolonged drought caused the District to take a "no annexation" position. Most directors have felt the district has more land than can presently be served, and have been reluctant to accommodate more annexation requests.

In an effort to reduce irrigation costs in Highland Valley avocado groves, a move was started in the late 1970s to find a way to buy raw, untreated water from the district. Property owners in that area approved a special assessment district to build a dual water system in 1980. This 22 miles of parallel lines cost $5 million to build and carries only raw water, thus saving the grower the unneccessary costs of treating irrigation water to drinking standards.

As available water resources have shrunk in relation to population growth over the years, San Diego County leaders have searched for ways and means to meet those demands. Historically, solutions were often found by building dams to increase storage capacity. But more often than not, those dams have been the cause of considerable controversy.

Three major dam projects have been planned for construction in the Ramona area. Two were built and are history. They are the Sutherland and Lake Ramona dams. However, ground has yet to broken on the third one, even though the land was acquired and plans begun on the Pamo Dam over 60 years ago.

Sutherland Dam

Thirty-five years elapsed between completion of Sutherland and completion of Lake Ramona, the last two major dams to be built in San Diego County. Those two projects not only share the honor of being located in the Ramona area, but also the dubious distinction of having been plagued by engineering errors, cost overruns and litigation.

Sutherland was started in 1927 when the City of San Diego agreed to acquire the Hodges and San Dieguito dams and reservoir lands in order to bolster their water resources. Additionally, the Sutherland and Pamo dam sites were acquired. A year later the voters of that city approved a $2 milion bond issue to construct a dam at the

Sutherland site and a diverting dam at San Vicente.
The Sutherland Dam had no sooner been started in 1928, than an investigation disclosed that part of the foundation was not safe and geologists recommended the site be moved 1,000 feet further upstream. The city engineer lost his job over that revelation. But before they could get the first few concrete sections finished, they'd run out of money. Land owners in the San Pasqual Valley challenged the City's right to impound the waters of the Santa Ysabel Creek and litigation dragged on. The Sutherland project lay dormant for 25 years.

When work was finally resumed in 1952, the old wooden forms on buttresses that had been poured in 1928 were still in place. As workers started removing those forms, thousands of bats flew out startling everyone.

Because of the high cost of constructing mulitple-arch dams, Sutherland was the last to be built in San Diego using that design. It is 161 feet high and can hold 29,000 acre feet of water.

Sutherland's waters were intended by the city to flow into their system through the San Vicente reservoir. However, since those plans were conceived in the 1920s, the county water authority was formed and began importing water from the Colorado River, which not only made more water available but also allowed more flexibility in raw water management.

In May 1952, recognizing an opportunity to gain a sorely needed new source of water, RID board president Oliver Garrett, wrote the City of San Diego requesting they consider letting Ramona use some of Sutherland's water. The RID offered to rejoin the CWA, and when that was accomplished they reasoned, Ramona could then exchange its aqueduct allotment for City water from the dam. This would save the RID the cost of having to build a line from the aqueduct. But according to Gary Butterfield, who became RMWD general manager in 1961, the city bureaucrates came up with excessively inflated surcharges. They made such a deal totally infeasible and nothing came of that proposal.

However, 12 years later, after the RMWD had been formed, becoming part of the authority, and had built their line to the aqueduct, an arrangement was finally agreed upon. The opportunity to save pumping costs was realized when the RMWD was able to negotiate an agreement in 1964 that involved a simple water swap. Because of Sutherland's higher elevation, trading some of Ramona's entitlement from the aqueduct for water from Sutherland has meant the difference between pumping those gallons uphill, or letting them flow downhill. Not only has Ramona benefited from lower operating costs, but the quality of water from Sutherland is generally superior.

In order to use Sutherland water, it had to be treated. Butterfield told of how his customers reacted when the district first started testing the delivery system from the dam. "Water was coming off the bottom of the lake and was dead, no oxygen in it. It really smelled and tasted badly." he recalled, "Tom Griffin called after two days of receiving that water and said, 'OK, I give up, you've had us hooked up to the sewer, now hook us back up to the water system.'"

Ramona voters approved a bond issue for $1.5 million to build a treatment plant which was completed in June 1974. The facility was named in honor of the father of Ramona's first water district, John C. Barger.

Lake Ramona

During the last part of the 1970s California was again experiencing one of its worst droughts in decades. By 1978 water was being rationed in communities all over the state. Lake Sutherland was nearly dry and other San Diego county reservoirs dangerously low.

The possibility of building Lake Ramona dam was first discussed as part of a RMWD master water plan in 1978. "It became apparent to those who studied the situation," said James Laughlin, "that Ramona could build hundreds of tanks and still not have enough storage. A large dam was the most cost effective answer." Laughlin had just been hired as the district's new general manager in early 1979. He suggested that the district investigate the feasibility of a low interest federal loan to finance such a project. Laughlin, with district directors Gordon Zick and John Wilson flew to Boulder City, Arizona to meet with U.S. Department of Interior officials and were encouraged with what they learned.

The board gave its unanimous vote to proceed, with members Oscar Pike, Ray Stock and Robert Shumate joining Zick and Wilson in the decision. An engineering firm specializing in such projects was hired to start preliminary plans and prepare the necessary applications for the federal loan. Early community supporters including Gene Gillett, Harold Clark and Peter Harrington were appointed in 1980 to serve as directors of a non-profit corporation to oversee the finance program.

Laughlin, flying his own airplane, had surveyed the territory and found what appeared to be five possible locations. The Green Valley Truck Trail location seemed to fit into the system best, and engineering studies confirmed the selection. It was situated near the district's existing pump station and in a deep canyon which could be economically dammed, yet hold a relatively high volume of water. This would also result in savings on land acquisition as well as evaporation once it was filled. Preliminary plans called for a lake that could hold up to 13,000 acre feet. However after several design changes, the finished capacity is 11,000 acre feet, or about 3.6 billion gallons of water.

In June 1981, district voters approved the project which called for obtaining a no-interest $19.6 million loan from the U.S. Bureau of Reclamation and floating two bond issues totaling $6.2 million for purchase of land.

But with President Ronald Reagan taking office that year, and the administration cutting back on public project funding, hopes dimmed for obtaining the key federal loan. Harold Schachter and Charles LeMenager had replaced Zick and Shumate on the RMWD board that year. Le-Menager, who earlier had served in Gov. Reagan's state administration, went to Washington and met with Interior Department officials and with Rep. Clair Burgener to see what could be done for the Ramona project.

It had been twenty years since any major dam was built in San Diego County. Additional capacity for safe water storage was not keeping pace with countywide growth. Burgener, a San Diegan, and highly respected member of the U.S. House of Representatives Appropriations Committee, was concerned and went to bat for the project, not only with his colleagues in the House but also with the Administration. One year, and many meetings, later Congressman Burgener was able to call with the good news: While the White House had stricken all but three dam projects from the budget, Ramona was one of those three survivors. Groundbreaking ceremonies were held in December 1982, and Clair Burgener tossed the first shovel of dirt.

Unfortunately, everything was not smooth sailing from there. The construction contract was awarded in November 1984, but the contractor walked off the job 13 months later, contending the firm hired to design the reservoir failed to provide an accurate estimate of excavation work. Construction ground to a halt. In early 1986 the RMWD board had to go back to the federal government for $6.4 million more to cover escalating costs.

GROUND BREAKING FOR LAKE RAMONA, DECEMBER 1982. Left to right: County Supervisor Paul Fordem, Congressman Clair Burgener, RMWD directors Oscar Pike, Harold Schachter, RMWD general manager James Laughlin, RMWD directors Ray Stock, Gordon Zick, board president Charles LeMenager and County Supervisor Paul Eckert.

Ramona Dam dedication August 1988. Civil War cannon salute from Charlie Marsh.

WATER STARTS COMING INTO LAKE RAMONA, SPRING 1989. What looks like a big hole in the ground, starts to take form as an 11,000 acre foot reservoir for life sustaining water, as well as a lake for recreation uses.

Meanwhile a citizens group asked for a grand jury investigation blaming mismanagement for the delays and mounting costs. The grand jury took up the matter but didn't find cause for serious action. There was talk by some of abandoning the project, but a majority of the board laid that question to rest by voting in June to go forward and advertise for new bids.

After being stalled for over a year, construction was resumed with a new general contractor in January 1987 and the dam finally finished in the summer of 1988. Dedication ceremonies were presided over in August by RMWD president Bernard Kuhn and general manager Jose Hurtado.

The original federal loan was predicated upon the district's high percentage of agricultural water sales. Federal officials had stipulated that reservoir water could be used only for agricultural use. In May 1988, the Federal Government offered the district a chance to pay off its $26 million loan for only $5.3 million, thus removing that restriction on water use. The district restructured the debt on the project, taking advantage of the discounted pay off, as well as gaining more flexibility in future water operations.

During the ten year period from 1979 to 1989, there was an abnormally high turnover of District officers. In that relatively short period of time, the position of general manager changed hands seven times, while 19 different directors have served on the five member board. In spite of this lack of countinuity, the community saw to it that the dam got finished, albeit two to three years late.

The Pamo Dam

The Pamo Dam project has been part of an overall water resource plan for the region for over 60 years. The project, if and when it is built, will create a reservoir providing emergency storage as well as operational fexibilty for the CWA. It will be capable of holding 130,000 acre feet of water, over 10 times the capacity of Lake Ramona. The major components of the plan are a 264-foot high roller-compacted concrete dam with built-in spillway, a 19-mile pipeline from the lake to the CWA's second aqueduct and a pipeline intertie with Lake Sutherland with a hydroelectric facility. Plans also call for facilities for fishing and picnicing.

However, after receiving approvals from the U.S. Army Corps of Engineers, and other State and Federal agencies in 1987, the project currently lies dormant, a victim of unresolved environmental issues. The CWA's position is that Federal requirements laid down for environmental mitigation are too costly to justify construction at this time. For the time being, other alternative sources of water and means for storage are being given higher priority than the proposed Pamo Dam.

16

Public Services

When the new Ramona Irrigation District brought water into Ramona's homes in 1926, most of the domestic water wells that existed in every back yard were no longer needed. They either became a hazard for some small child to fall in, if not sealed; or they provided a practical use. That practical use turned out to be a new household cesspool. Rather than go to the time and expense of digging a new hole when the present one got filled, the privy was simply moved over onto the old well.

It thus became only a matter of time before the "privey and cesspool" method of wastewater disposal would become another problem for the growing town. The old well located behind the Masonic Temple, for example, not only served as a cesspool for the lodge but for several adjoining stores and shops as well. When it filled-up, as it did after a few months, it had to be pumped out. And it was. Right into an open ditch which flowed all the way down to 12th Street.

This practice was not uncommon throughout the back country, right up into the 1950s. In fact the City of Coronado was still pumping raw sewage into San Diego Bay into the 1960s.

After enough citizens raised enough cane, however, county government finally stepped in and formed the Ramona Sanitation District in 1950. The first sewer plant was built in Santa Maria Valley soon after, a crude plant by today's standards. It employed a tricking filter design that took all the ingenuity and skill the county's best plant operator could muster to keep it from smelling most of the time. But it was a decided improvement over what the town had before.

That plant had to be removed to a different location, however, when county officials became concerned with its close proximity to the RMWD's well fields, just 300' north. The town had outgrown the plant's capacity as well, and a citizens committee was formed in 1968 to advise on an expanded service area and new plant location.

The outcome of that study resulted in the county adopting a district boundary that roughly corresponded with the town center, and construction of a new wastewater treatment and disposal facility located further west in the Santa Maria Valley.

RMWD Branches Out

By and large, and in spite of its ups and downs, the RMWD has done an admirable job of keeping pace with the water needs of a fast growing Ramona. Not only that, but the district has also stepped in and provided additional public services as needed. In many respects, this district has developed into a municipal government. In the unincorporated area known as Ramona, it has been able to provide many local services normally expected from a city, with the exception of police, roads and land use regulation.

The RMWD now owns and operates two sanitation systems, one serving the Santa Maria Valley and another the San Vicente Valley. These operations are relatively new ventures for the District, both becoming a part of the RMWD within the past 17 years.

The developer of the planned community of San Diego Country Estates, built the San Vicente system to serve that 3,250 acre development. It was designed and built to RMWD and state specifications. The district took it over in 1973, excercising latent powers under the state Local Agency Formation Act. The original improvements included over 52 miles of collection lines serving the entire development, and a waste water treatment and disposal facility sized to accommodate the first ten years of build out. The plant facilities have been expanded once to meet growth demands and are currently being expanded again to meet the ultimate build out. Capital improvements and operating costs have been paid solely by those property owners.

In 1980, the RMWD again exercised latent powers when it took over the San Diego County Ramona Sanitation District which serves the Santa Maria Valley.

Fire Protection

In the early days Ramona, as most other small communities, had no organized fire protection. When a fire occurred, neighbors pitched in and hopefully put it out before everything was lost.

The earliest reference to Ramona attempting to form a fire department is found in a June 1914 edition of the Sentinel. It was reported that a Volunteer Fire Department organizing meeting was held and a committee was formed to "ascertain the cost of two ladders and a light truck to carry them." Another committee consisting of J.P. Sutherland, L.C. Janeway and W.E. Banks was to draft a constitution and

RAMONA'S FIRST PIECE OF FIRE FIGHTING EQUIPMENT. This soda-ash fire extinguisher was donated to the community by John Barger in 1924. Standing next to it at the Guy B. Woodward Museum are the current fire chief, Karl Diekman and department deputy chief Mike Neill.

by-laws. Apparently the program didn't get off the ground. Nothing can be found in the records of any concrete accomplishment for another 10 years.

As was the case with so many other public service needs in the beginning, it was John Bargar and the Chamber of Commerce who first got something done about fire protection.

Bargar suggested the Chamber board set up a volunteer fire department in 1924 and he donated a soda ash fire extinguisher from his lumber yard to help provide the first piece of equipment. He also furnished the fire alarm in the form of an old railroad engine tire. This was a large steel ring hung from a post, which when struck with a sledge hammer could be heard all over the valley. This old ring was later replaced with a more modern siren, but had to be put back into use again during World War II because the siren had to be reserved for air raid warnings.

ONE OF JOHN BARGAR'S OLD CONSTRUCTION TRUCKS. This was donated to the community in 1927 and converted into its first fire truck by adding a tank and some ladders.

In 1927 Bargar donated a used Reo truck, which with a 50 gallon tank on the bed, served as a water tanker. Soon thereafter, Charley Weseloh who owned the Chevrolet agency in town, donated a 1923 Dodge truck. It was equipped with 600 feet of two and a half inch hose and a couple of ladders supplied by the County.

With two old trucks and a scant collection of equipment to work with, an organized fire department began to take form. John Bargar again became another Ramona first, its first fire chief.

Other non-paid chiefs to follow included William "Bill" Cannon, who served from 1928 to 1931, "Cap" Williams from 1931 to about 1942, Claude Oates followed by Jack Jones who served until 1950 when Ramona hired its first paid fire fighter. He was Chief Erwin Bernhard who stayed for two years. Others who have since served as Ramona Fire Chief include Ed Eller, Rick Robertson, Bill Wright, Dan Williams, Von Rupple, John Allen and the present Chief Karl Diekman.

Bill Hanigan served for over 50 years as a commissioner or director of Ramona's fire department. He was one of the original members of the committee of Fire Department Affairs appointed by the Chamber of Commerce. That was in 1931 when their directors decided to formalize an organization to direct the fire department's activities. Other commissioners, as they were called on that first board were Charley Westloh, T.S. Hewlett, George Kayser and L.P. Coddington.

In a 1978 interview with Elrena Warnes, Hanigan said he figured he knew why the Chamber asked him to serve on that first board, "because as high school principal, I could get some of the district's typing business done free in Mrs. Ruth Shaw's typing class, and I did."

Financing of that fledgling department was by popular subscription and students typed the letters requesting donations. Hanigan personally donated $9 for postage that first year because there was nothing in the budget for the necessary three cent stamps. Annual donations for the fire department ran from a total of a few hundred dollars to as high as twelve hundred in those depression years.

Hanigan stayed active in Ramona fire protection until the RFPD was dissolved and made a part of the RMWD in 1981.

In the late 1940s, Ramona distiguished itself as being the first small town fire operation in California to be radio equipped for communications. By 1952 the district had approved plans for its first permanent fire station which still stands at 9th near Main. The contract which was let was not for a complete facility, but for an apparatus room to house three engines, an office and a partially complete squad room. The contract price was $7,500. Volunteer firemen completed the improvements on weekends and nights at an additional cost to the taxpayers of less than $600.

THE FIRST PERMANENT FIRE STATION ON 9TH NEAR MAIN. Still in use today, it was build in 1952 for less than $9,000 cost to Ramona taxpayers. Much of the interior finish work was done by volunteer fire fighters. Chief Eller is shown standing on far left with his volunteer department in 1957.

Chief Bernhard was instrumental in setting up a fire prevention program as well as leading the drive for a permanent fire station. Up until 1952, the trucks were housed on property loaned by civic minded people who allowed the volunteers to erect shelters for the equipment. However, when those properties were needed by the owners for other purposes, a new shelter had to be constructed elsewhere. It got to the point, according to William "Bill" Keyes Hanigan, that the fire commissioners were considering building a shed with skids so it could be saved and moved when they were next evicted.

While Ramona has had a fire protection program since the 1920s, it did not operate as a formal tax supported governmental agency until 1946. That was the year the Ramona Fire Protection District was formed. Up until that time, fire protection came from private contributions and volunteers. Assessed valuation was $2 million for that first year the RFPD went into operation.

Until the 1970s the only paid firefighter was the chief. But when the 3,250 acre planned community of San Diego Country Estates annexed into the RFPD, providing a big boost to the town's assessed valuation, the department shifted from primarily volunteer firefighters to a paid staff. When the developer of San Diego Country Estates annexed into the district, he agreed to donate a fire station, including land and equipment. That facility cost about $125,000 and was completed in 1974. Today, plans are in place for another station to be built on Dye Road near Highway 67. This will bring to three the number of facilities providing structural fire protection for the area.

In 1978, the voters of California passed a constitutional referendum, know as Proposition 13, the Jarvis-Gann Initiative. This new law limited the amount local jurisdictions could increase property taxes. As a result, Ramona's small fire department was left with little in the way of a tax rate to keep pace with the town's exploding growth. It had no legal power to impose assessments or fees. A provision in the state municipal water code, however, allowed water districts to charge fees for fire protection, and it became apparent that if the fire department became part of the district, it would be in a better position to provide the ways and means to meet its growing obligation to the community.

In May 1981, the Ramona Fire Protection District directors voted to dissolve, and the RMWD directors voted to take over the fire department. With this change, structural fire protection became available to all within the RMWD boundaries thus expanding the service area from 17,000 to nearly 47,000 acres.

There are as of 1989, a total of 30 full time, and 19 reserve fire department employees. The department also contracts for two full time ambulances and six paramedic technicians.

FRED GRAND, THE MAN WHO PLAYED A LEADING ROLE in development of the Ramona community park. His hard work, along with that of dozens of other volunteers have turned the RMWD's well fields into an outstanding community park and fairgrounds at very little cost to the taxpayers.

Parks and Recreation

Another public service operated to some extent under the RMWD's organizational umberella is a local park and recreation program. This all began because the water district had dozens of acres available in its well fields which were ideally suited for recreation purposes.

This has resulted in development and operation of ball fields, arenas, fair buildings and an outdoor center by a public/private sector partnership. While leadership, labor and much of the material needed to build the facilities has come from community volunteers, the district has been supportive by making the land available and providing some administrative services and capital improvements.

Always in the forefront when needed, and providing leadership and organizational drive was Fred Grand. He had moved to Ramona in the 1960s from the Julian area, where the Grand family had been prominent for generations. Grand was a past president of the Julian Chamber of

Commerce where he helped get the annual Julian Apple Festival Days started in 1949. Once in Ramona, that same energy and community spirit was turned to helping develop fairground and park facilities. He holds an honorary life membership in the Ramona Chamber of Commerce in recognition of his many contributions.

Others whose effort and dedication has made the difference between success and failure in local park, fair and 4-H programs include the Zicks, Donna and Gordon; Rod Jerde, George Boggs, Maria and Charley Steiner, the Tobiasons, Angus and Art; Emma Schmidt, Peggy Rice, Brian Evers, Art Thomson and many others, too numerous to list. The results of their collective efforts have added up to a comprehensive program that is found in very few communities of similar size.

In 1979 the RMWD went after a share of County Community Block Grant funds for creation of a community center. With County Supervisor Paul Eckert's help and support, Ramona was able to receive an allocation of about $300,000. As a result, the 7,300 square foot center, which is located adjacent to the fair grounds, became a reality and was dedicated in 1978. It serves not only as a community senior citizens center, where over 240 luncheons are currently being prepared daily, but provides meeting space for other public purposes.

Move Toward Cityhood

During the early 1980s, a formal movement was started to incorporate Ramona as a city. Leaders in this move, who included Oscar Pike, David Ross and Lee Weddington, pointed to what they felt was a lack of responsiveness on the part of the county board of supervisors toward local needs and desires. While the primary concern centered on land use matters, it was also felt by some that Ramona as a city, could provide a better level of services for less cost to its taxpayers. The move was aimed at putting the matter before the voters on the June 1982 ballot. State law, however, requires that a county Local Agency Formation Commission (LAFCO) approve such elections, and only after an analysis proves the fiscal viability of such a move. A two year budget was prepared for the proposed "Township" (a term that proponents chose to call the proposed city) but it failed to convince LAFCO. The commission felt that cityhood for Ramona was premature for the time, and the hoped for election didn't came to pass.

Community Planning Groups

Some of the local pressure for incorporation has been relieved in recent years by a change in the county board of supervisors' attitude toward local desires as expressed by the Ramona Community Planning Group.

But that was not always the case. About 1973, the County of San Diego began developing community master plans in the various unicorporated towns. Ramona was a prime candidate for such planning and for county staff assistance. Unfortunately, Ramona was number seven on the schedule, far down on the county's priority list, and it seemed nobody in the county was pushing to help Ramona any sooner.

In preparing those community plans, the county was setting up local citizen groups which received official recognition as planning advisors. Several Ramona citizens were not satisfied to just sit by and wait for three or four years until the planning department decided to get around to Ramona. They formed their own planning group to force the issue. Included in this grass-roots move were Oscar Pike, Tom Griffin, Bill Jones, Vern Leming, Gary Kesselring, Ruth Meyer and Marvin Patcher. According to Tom Griffin, the group started its own planning studies, keeping pressure on county staff, until the county got the picture and moved the Ramona Community Plan schedule to the top of the list.

Soon after, community planning groups were formed in all the major unicorporated areas of the county and given legal status through the election process. These committees consist of 15 members elected at large, and have the responsibilty for reviewing and advising on general plans and other county land use matters affecting the community.

With County recognition and formalization of the process, community input is supposed to carry more weight. However, that has not always been the case. Such committees can have considerable influence, or little, depending on the political climate and make-up of the board of supervisors. It is the board that has the ultimate decision making authority. Some previous supervisors all but ignored local groups, while some have acted like rubber stamps.

Until recently, because earlier boards of supervisors seemed not to give enough weight to the Ramona group's advise, few people ran for seats on the RCPG, and most openings were filled by appointment. However, the 1988 election found more Ramona candidates than there were openings. At the request of the county, the group has been involved in an increasingly wider range of planning issues facing their community.

Airport

Ramona's present airport located on Monticito Road is a far cry from the town's first landing field which consisted of a 1,000 foot runway and one small metal hanger. It was carved out on Art Stockton's place in 1939, who according to Frank Kunkel, "was tickled to death to be able to watch the planes land and take off there." That first facility was

RAMONA'S FIRST AIRPORT. Two of the town's early flyers were Glen Zentz and Gordon Kunkel pictured in front of a Taylorcraft in 1939. The landing field was located on the west bank of Santa Maria Creek south of 10th Street.

nestled along the southwest side of Santa Maria Creek near 10th Street. The Kunkel brothers, Gordon and Frank thought they'd like to learn to fly about that time, and with the help of their father Watson, bought a 40 horse power Piper Cub for $800. That plane was to be the means for several other local flying aspirants to solo in Ramona in those pre World War II days.

That first landing field was closed on the day the Japanese attacked Pearl Harbor, never to reopen. But the U.S. Navy had completed a $500,000 auxiliary landing field toward the end of the war located less than three miles southwest of town. The Navy field, with its 4,000 foot long runway was not being used in 1946. Gordon Kunkel, who had been a flight instructor for the Air Corps, and Glen Zentz who had been shot down and spent time in a German prisoner of war camp, made a deal to set up a flight operation on the new facility. Zentz and Kunkel became Ramona's first fixed base operators. By August 1946 they presided over seven small planes based at the facility.

The County of San Diego leased the base from the Navy

ANTIQUE BIPLANES TODAY SHARE THE RAMONA AIRPORT WITH
FIRE FIGHTING HELICOPTERS AND BOMBERS AS WELL AS THE MORE
COMMON GENERAL AVIATION PLANES.

in 1947 and bought it in 1957 under Public Law 287. Since
that time there have been several County base operators
including Erwin Nielsen and "Pinkie" Pinkerton.

In 1979 Ron MacKenzie took over and still has an interest in the operation although the name has since been
changed to Pacific Executive Aviation. There are now also
two more private aviation operations in business on the
base. They are Cruisair Aviation on the south side of the
field and Chuck Hall Aviation on the west end. Between
the three operations, Ramona Airport now is home to over
175 private general aviation aircraft, a far cry from the
seven planes based there in 1946.

The Ramona airport is also home to the California
Division of Forestry and U.S. Forest Service joint fire
fighting air attack operation for San Diego County. They
provide skilled pilots and fire fighting planes during the
fire season and put out many brush fires before they have
a chance to do serious damage to homes in the area.

17

Agri-Business

From the time the white man first set foot in what is now San Diego county, raising cattle has always been a major industry in the back country. Even today, with many of the old rancho lands overgrown with housing development, there remains a cattle empire still doing business where George Sawday started it in Witch Creek in 1904.

George Sawday was a living legend among cattlemen for most of the first half of this century. He was the son of Englishman Frederick R. Sawday who came to the Julian area shortly after gold was discovered and went into business as a storekeeper and freight wagon operator. The elder Sawday moved his operations to Witch Creek in 1881 where he did a thriving business serving the traffic between San Diego and the mines. F.R. Sawday eventually moved on to Ensenada, Baja California where he owned and operated a large mercantile store for his last 25 years.

While in Witch Creek, the family became acquainted with the another English family, the Herbert Crouchs who were running large flocks of sheep through the back

THE F.R. SAWDAY RESIDENCE, STORE AND STAGE STOP, Witch Creek 1882.

country. Young George met one of the Herbert Crouch's daughters, Emily and in 1904 the two were married. He built the home that stands today, by greatly enlarging his parent's house with lumber he purchased for $200 from the Witch Creek Church which was no longer being used. That home still serves today as the headquarters of a vast cattle operation stretching over large portions of San Diego County and being run by third and forth generation members of the family.

At its peak, George Sawday's cattle operation numbered several thousand head. Some newspaper accounts had it as large as 10,000 head, but according to Mrs. Lucy Cumming, "It was more like eight thousand." Lucy is George's daughter, and together with husband Orville Cumming took over the operation in 1949 when George passed away. Lucy's and Orville's children and grandchildren now run the far ranging enterprise.

GEORGE SAWDAY. A cattleman and industry leader renown throughout the country.

George Sawday once also owned and grazed cattle on the 8,500 acre Los Penasquitos Rancho which now houses tens of thousands San Diego city folk. Besides Witch Creek, Sawday descendants still run cattle on the San Felipe Ranch, Coogan Ranch, Rancho Cuyamaca, Cameron Ranch, Crouch Meadows as well as several thousands of Bureau of Land Management acres which it leases. They also operate a feed lot in Imperial Valley.

The Turkey Capital of the World

For over thirty years, during the 1930s through the 1950s, Ramona was known as the Turkey Capital of the World.

On a hot dry summer day, a traveler driving in the San Diego County back country knew he was approaching Ramona when he saw large clouds of dust on the horizon, dust scratched up by thousands of Santa Maria Valley turkeys and being carried airborne by the prevailing westerly winds.

In the early part of the 1920s, however, Santa Maria Valley was more or less typical when it came to turkey raising. But three or four ranchers saw the possibilities and

PRESIDENT HARRY TRUMAN ACCEPTING PRIZE WINNING TURKEY
from local industry leader Albert Matlock on far right and other
industry association officers. Picture taken about 1949

began experimenting with small flocks. The turkey business rocked along until about 1928 when a few others caught on to some of the pluses Ramona offered in the way of growing conditions. It seems the Ramona area had an advantage over other turkey raising areas. It had a climate which encouraged the birds to lay earlier in the year. Turkeys were laying eggs in Ramona as early as November while growers in the east and mid-west couldn't expect their hens to lay until May or June.

Ramona was able to turn this advantage into an industry that, during the depression, accounted for annual sales of 1,200,000 turkey eggs being sold at the astounding price of over 21 cents each. And this was in 1936, when chicken eggs were selling for 18 cents a dozen. By bringing in eggs from Ramona during the winter and early spring, eastern growers were able get their flocks started and ready for market four to six months earlier.

TURKEY FEATHER DRESS FOR ANNUAL TURKEY DAY CELEBRATION. Mary Kay Holly Pinkard shown about 1947 is still active in Ramona community promotion. Mary Kay was Ramona honorary mayor 1986-87 and presently serves as Chamber of Commerce secretary.

Selling the eggs was more profitable than raising the birds since the growers were able to save on the high cost of grain for fattening the turkeys for meat. However, many birds were indeed raised for their meat. The local broad breasted variety was developed from stock found in Oregon in 1936 and the "Ramona Broad-breasted Mountain Brand" was famous for its quality. Local growers also had a big business going in selling poults, newly hatched birds which were shipped to growers in the colder climes. Sycamore Fields, a cooperative hatchery located in Goose Valley, as one example, shipped 10,000 poults per truck load twice a week to Utah. No wonder Ramona was known as the "Turkey Capital of the World".

In 1933, Ramona growers formed their own association and by 1936 had over 90 members. During that year more than 80,000 birds were grown and dressed in the valley.

At its height in 1950, the association boasted 123 members, which included a few growers from Lakeside and El Cajon. Eggs were being shipped at the rate of a million and a quarter annually and selling for as high as 62 cents each, FOB Ramona, while local plants processed and sold two million pounds of dressed meat. There were two large meat processing plants in the valley where turkeys were killed, dressed and packaged as fresh, frozen or smoked. One plant was run by Fred Gleeson on Main Street and the other by Harold K. Darling, a pioneer in the Ramona turkey industry for over forty years.

Darling started raising and processing turkeys in 1921, and during that first year raised only 500 birds. By the 1930's and 40's when his plant was running at its peak, he would process up to 1,000 birds a day. The peak months were from August to February, and Darling did a big business for the government during Wold War II.

During those halcyon days of the turkey, Ramona held its grand 'Turkey Day" festival each year on the first Saturday in November and thousands of people came from far and wide to attend the festivities. There was a parade, turkey show with judging, booths for food and games and free turkeys given away. This was held in Collier Park and turkey growers from all over southern California entered their prize birds in the contests.

One of the high-lights of Turkey Day was the flavorful smoked turkey that was served. Smoking turkeys is a delicate art, and one of Ramona's leading growers knew how to do it in a grand style. Out on the Frank Denison ranch near Air Mail Lane, they used nothing but lemon wood which they burned at the base of a giant bee-hive shaped smoke oven. Fifty birds at a time were placed on metal bars and the cooking process went on for two days and two nights.

Like most good things, time has a way of changing the

game and the way it is played. Ramona's days of being "Turkey Capital" ground to a halt in the early 1960s. The turkey egg business went sour when eastern growers learned how to stimulate their own birds into laying early, and the poult business was taken over by the big feed companies which were able to meet that demand more competitively. A booming San Diego County also brought higher land prices and property taxes, and that meant higher and more prohibitive costs for raising grain for feed.

Avocados

Orchards and crops have historically played a prime roll in the Santa Maria Valley agriculture. But as more and more people came to build homes, the relative value of land for residential development has made it extremely hard for the small farmer to survive. Coupled with high land costs and property taxes, the high cost of water is slowly but surely diminishing the role agriculture plays in the area.

Avocado farming in Highland Valley enjoyed tremendous popularity during the later 1970s and early 1980s. Primarily because of two factors: a product that usually brings high prices in relation to most other crops, and favorable income tax treatment allowed under the U.S. Internal Revenue Code during that period in time. Many growers could shelter income while watching the value of their land increase along with other San Diego real estate. With changes in the law, however, many of the attractive tax advantages have been eliminated from the code.

While avocados continue to be a profitable product in other parts of the county, Ramona growers however, are finding it harder to make them pay because of the high cost for water. Ramona growers pay more because their water must be pumped up hill from the County Water Authority's aqueduct. And even with the dual system which allows them to save the costs of treatment, water is still much higher than in Escondido and other areas located at lower elevations.

For two winters in a row, 1987 and 1988, extended hard frosts have also played havoc with local growers. It has been estimated that as much as 15 to 20 percent of the established trees were lost in those frosts and most weren't replanted.

Many predict that if San Diego County continues to grow at its current pace, Highland Valley will see much more residential development and less agriculture in the not too distant future.

One grower who found it more profitable to sell his land than to replant after those frosts was David Galusa. "Some of us who were in the same boat formed a small support group." Galusa said, "We called it 'AA', avocados anonymous. Whenever someone talked about replanting, we'd sit down and drink with him until he got over the urge."

Not all Highland Valley growers have found avocados to be a marginal business, however. Charlie Snow is an industry pioneer, and one of the more successful growers in the Ramona area. Snow has about 10,000 trees, but doesn't rely totally upon district water. He started planting back in the early 1960s and has been able to develop wells that provide a high percentage of his irrigation needs.

It is estimated that there are over 150,000 avocado trees in Highland Valley. (RMWD dual water system sales have averaged 4,200 acre feet annually for the past three years. With 2.75 af of district water purchased per acre per year on the average, planted acreage would total about 1,525 acres, times 100 trees per acre gives us the .15 million figure.)

While not extensive by Highland Valley standards, plantings are found in other parts of Ramona. According to Warren Henry, who has a grove in Goose Valley, there are currently about 125 acres of trees in that area. But water costs are even

COMBINE CREW MOVED FROM ONE RAMONA AREA VALLEY TO ANOTHER AT HARVEST TIME. This crew is shown working in a barley field in the San Vicente Valley about 1912. Dry grain farming took place throughout the Santa Maria, Pamo, Goose and Ballena Valleys, and these contract crews moved from one field to the next. On Saturday nights they came home for a bath and some relaxation. During the week they worked sun-up to sun-down sleeping with the horses and equipment at night.

higher there than in Highland Valley because untreated water is not available. Henry is not sure how much longer anyone can afford to operate there and he predicts that most of those trees will be gone in a year or so.

On the other end of the cost spectrum, the Solk Ranch located on the western edge of San Vicente Valley enjoys much lower water rates than any other district customer. In 1983 these growers were able to negotiate a deal with the RMWD to buy the treated effluent that was being wasted at the San Vicente treatment facility. The grower agreed to pay the capital costs of pumping, transmission and storage facilities to handle the increased flows at the plant. In exchange they are able to buy the effluent at a relatively low rate. While this is projected to save the grower a great deal of money in the long run, the district was saved the up-front costs of acquiring additional expensive land and equipment for wastewater disposal.

Original expansion plans for the San Vicente system called for the plant's treated effluent to ultimately be pumped back up the valley for use on the San Vicente golf course. But when the time came for expansion in 1982, however, the District was short of funds and the Estates' association could not justify the costs of providing the necessary facilities and equipment. That's when the growers stepped in.

This was the district's first viable reclamation program and was considered a progressive, 'win-win deal' for both parties at the time.

18

Ramona Today

THE CHAMBER OF COMMERCE'S BIG ANNUAL EVENT IS THE CASEY TIBBS RODEO, which draws entries and spectators from all over the country.

THE FOURTH OF JULY PARADE IN SAN DIEGO COUNTRY ESTATES, inspires neighborhood competition for the most original float. The 1989 winner with this "Little Red Schoolhouse" creation was the Matlin Road group.

RAMONA'S OLIVE PEIRCE MIDDLE SCHOOL ON HANSON LANE.
By 1994-95 school year the Ramona Unified School District student enrollment, kindergarten through 12th grade, exceeded 6,600 students. This compares with but 1,500 students in 1968-69. The rapid growth in District population required an extensive school expansion program that saw four new schools added in the District in just six years. James Dukes Elementary was opened in 1985, Olive Peirce Middle School in 1986, Woodson Elementary, 1989 and Barnett Elementary in 1991. All three were named in honor of leading Ramona pioneers. Currently (1995) there are six elementary, one middle, one high school and one alternative school (7 through 12) in the District.

GENEVA AND GUY WOODWARD STANDING IN THE BANCROFT GARDEN IN FRONT OF THE VERLAQUE HOUSE. Theophile Verlaque, a prosperous San Diego businessman, built his country home next to his son's store in 1886. The house was donated to the Ramona Pioneer Historical Society by the Ransom family in 1984. With the leadership of the Woodward, this home and its grounds have been converted into one of the finest small town museums in the country.

RAMONA TOWN HALL celebrated it's 100th anniversary when it was placed on the National Register of Historic Places in September 1994. This honor came after several years of effort by local Ramona Town Hall Association leaders in raising funds and restoring the grand old lady. Shown here freshly restored to the way she appeared when finished in February 1894. Only difference being today's paved sidewalk, street, curb and gutter, and the absence of a library sign over the left wing denoting the main reason for Martha Barnett's support for this family donation to the community.

THIS CONGREGATIONAL CHURCH BUILDING IS OVER 80 YEARS OLD. It was dedicated in February 1907. The church started meeting in temporary quarters in 1898 and today is the oldest active church group in Ramona. Until 1987, however, when it was desolved, the Friends Church organization held that distinction, having been formed in the mid-1880s. Today there are 22 organized Christian groups and one Jewish Synagogue meeting regularly in the Ramona area.

THE JUNIOR LIVESTOCK FAIR AND 4-H COMPETITION are big events every year for Ramona's youth. Proud 4-H winners in the poultry division are Desiree Donahoe and Rebecca Walter.

RAMONA'S OLDEST STORE, AS IT LOOKS TODAY. Built in 1883 by Amos Verlaque as a general store and post office for the new settlement of Nuevo, this building is still housing retail business on Ramona's main drag.

SAL'S PLUMBING AND HARDWARE STANDS TODAY where Creelman's blacksmith shop and Coddington's garage stood in earlier days.

THE OLD TELEPHONE COMPANY RESTAURANT, was one of Ramona's first main street restoration projects in 1987. Current plans call for revitalization of the old center section of Main Street to bring back the charm and character of earlier Ramona.

THE RAMONA SENTINEL, STILL DOING BUSINESS ON MAIN STREET. But the computer age has taken over from the old ways of composing, setting type and printing. Today, while the editorial, advertising and management staff still work in Ramona, the paper is printed at the parent company's plant in Poway.

RAMONA IS WELL REPRESENTED WITH SERVICE CLUBS AND FRATERNAL ORGANIZATIONS. The Ramona Women's Club has been active since 1912 and has its own clubhouse on Main Street. Ramona Rotary goes back to 1937. They used to hold their meetings at the Kennelworth Inn where lunches cost 50 cents and the usual fine was 10 cents.

COMMUNITY CENTER BUILDING. Built in 1978, it serves mainly as a senior citizen's center. Since the Town Hall was shut down, however, it has provided a meeting place for a wide variety of other groups.

RAMONA DRUGGISTS HAVE BEEN IN THE FOREFRONT FOR OVER 100 YEARS. Bryan Woods,(r) is doing business at the same location as was the Jerman family a century ago. Seated is John Fansher, Ramona's honorary mayor 1987-88, who bought the store in 1933 and sold it to Gordon Zick in 1966, who in turn sold to Woods in 1982. Like Lem Jerman before him, Zick served on the Ramona water board, while Woods is a past president of the C of C and serves on the local planning group. Fansher and Zick still help Woods in the pharmacy on occasion.

SAN VICENTE GOLF COURSE WAS OPENED IN FEBRUARY 1973. It was Ramona's first course, built as part of the planned community of San Diego Country Estates. Shown is the author's wife Nancy teeing off. Spangler Peak is in the background.

Epilogue

Ramona put on a centennial celebration in 1986 with much fanfare. That year coincided with the 100th anniversary of the purchase of land by the Santa Maria Land and Water Company and the beginning of their subdivision of 3,853 acres for home and farm sites which they called "Ramona".

But from the time Verlaque established his store in 1883 until the postoffice was renamed "Ramona" in June 1895 all San Diego County government records and County and City directories referred to the little town in Santa Maria Valley as "Nuevo". And well into 1895, newspaper advertising referred to the "Nuevo Town Hall", J.A. Verlaque billed himself as "The Pioneer Merchant of Nuevo" and "THOMAS JERMAN, Druggist, dealer in Drugs, Medicines and Chemicals and Patent Medicines", claimed to be doing business in no place but Nuevo.

Even though some wished it to be Ramona, businessmen and government officials didn't refer to the town as such until the post office department changed the name.

RAMONA'S 1970 CELEBRATION MEDALIONS. Antique bronze sold for $2.50 and the .990 silver for $10.50.

But, believe it or not, the 1986 event wasn't "Ramona's" first 100th anniversary celebration. Seems that back in 1970, a couple of Chamber of Commerce leaders with lots of drive, imagination and enthusiasm thought it was time for a Ramona Centennial celebration.

Never mind the fact that in 1870 there was nothing in the whole of the Santa Maria Valley but a few hundred head of Stokes' cattle grazing peacefully; not even a suggestion of commercial, residential or cultural development in the Valley. A celebration was a great way to promote the town and have a bit of fun at the same time. They even made up and sold silver and bronze centennial coins to prove that Ramona was 100 years old.

So what? No harm done. We're not the only town that's jumped the gun. Coronodo has also had two centennial celebrations and is planning a third right now.

Look at it this way. It just means that if Coronado can get away with doing it three times, we should be able to do it too. June 1995 will mark the 100th anniversary of when business and government officially recognized us as

Ramona and stopped calling us Nuevo. Seems to me that should be as good a reason for a Ramona Centennial as the ones used for the last two.

And surely, some day Ramona will incorporate as a city, which means we could even have a fourth 100th birthday based on that event. (Lets just hope nobody changes the town name in the meantime.)

References & Resources

In researching this book I have drawn extensively from items published in our local newspaper, The Sentinel. We want to express thanks to the current publisher, Duane Spencer for his gracious help and cooperation with all of us involved in Ramona history.

We are deeply in debt to all those Ramona Pioneer Historical Society volunteers who have spent countless hours cataloging news items and other local historical documents. This work has made it much easier for those attempting to piece together parts of the jig-saw puzzle we call local history.

Additionally, I have drawn heavily from past editions of the San Diego Union. The California Room of the San Diego City Main Library has a microfiche index by subject for past editions 1851-1903 and 1930-1975. This source is rich in back country news items.

As a part of its vast collection of books and documents, the San Diego Historical Society has a fine collection of early San Diego County records. In 1987 they published "*A Guide to the San Diego Historical Society Public Records Collection*" by Richard W. Crawford. Those who are interested in local history may use this fine library of books, documents and photos by joining the Society or paying an admission charge per visit. The archives are located in Balboa Park.

The California State Library in Sacramento, maintains a microfilm library of old newspapers from throughout the state. Their collection includes copies of "The Sentinel" while it was published in Julian from December 1887 through December 1889, as well as copies published in Nuevo and Ramona from June 1893 to December 1904. But many issues are missing, and while very helpful, the collection is not complete.

Bibliography

Ashley, George, Letter dated November 7, 1966, (Ramona Pioneer Historical Society)

Bancroft, Hubert H., *History of California, Vols.I-VII* (San Francisco, The History Company, 1886),

Barger, John C., *The Ramona Irrigation District, Recompilation From the Beginning,* (Handwritten Account, Ramona Pioneer Historical Society Collection, 1938)

Bellon, Walter and Lane, Fred T., *Condensed History of San Diego County Park System,* (San Diego County Publication, 1944)

Bernhard, Edwin C., *Ramona Fire Chief's Annual Report, 1952,* (Ramona, Ramona Fire Department, 1952)

Brackett, R. W., *The History of San Diego County Ranchos,* (San Diego, Calif.,Title Insurance and Trust Company, 1974)

Carrico, Richard, *The San Diego County Indian Reservations of 1870,* (San Diego, Calif.,Brand Book Number Seven, The San Diego Corral of Westerners, 1983)

Cesa, Julio, *Recollections of My Youth at San Luis Rey Mission,* (Los Angeles, Touring Topics, So. Calif. Auto Club, Nov.1930)

Chamberlin, Eugene K.,Ph.D., *Santa Ysabel Asistencia,(1818-1987), Plaque Dedication Booklet,* (Squibob Chapter 1853, E Clampus Vitus, 1987)

Couts, Cave J., *The Journal and Maps of CJC, From SD to the Colorado in 1849,* (Los Angeles, Arthur M. Ellis, 1932)

Cowgill, Jane, collection, *Edward Stokes' Sea Logs,* San Diego.

Couro, Ted, *San Diego County Indians as Farmers and Wage Earners,* (Ramona Pioneer Historical Society, 1975)

Dana, Richard Henry, *Two Years Before The Mast,* (Various publishers, original published 1840)

Engelhardt, Fr. Zephyrin, *San Diego Mission,* (San Francisco, The James H. Berry Co., 1920)

Emory, W. H. Lt., *Notes of a Military Reconnoissance,* (Thirtieth Congress-First Session, Washington, D.C.,1848)

Escondido Times-Advocate, Article About Sutherland Dam Dedication Plans, 1/09/54 edition.

Fitch, Captain Henry, *Letters of a Merchant,* (Bancroft Library, University of California)

Fletcher, Col. Ed, *Memoirs of Ed Fletcher*, (San Diego, Pioneer Printers, 1952)

Frary, Maud Thayer, 1934 Interview, by W. Davidson, San Diego Historical Society Collection

Goodyear, W. A., *California State Mining Bureau Report*, (Sacramento, 1888)

Guinn, J. M., *A History of California and an Extended History of Its Southern California Coast Counties*, (Los Angeles, Historic Record Company, Los Angeles, 1907)

Hanigan, Lucile Keyes, Interview by Edger Hasting, September 11, 1958, Ramona, Ramona Pioneer Historical Society Collection

Hanigan, William Keyes, *History of Ramona Fire Department,and Early High School*, Interview by Elrena D. Warnes, Tape recording, September 1978, Ramona High School Library

Hayes, Judge Benjamin, *Pioneer Notes from the Diaries of,1849-1975*, (Los Angeles, Private Printing,1920)

Hughes, Charles, *The Decline of the Californios, 1846-1856*, Masters Thesis, (San Diego, California State University, 1972)

Jasper, James, *Julian and Round-About*, Typescript, 1928, Cynthia Kunckel Collection

Kerr, Cptn. Wm. M., *Notes on California Land Titles, Vol V*, Santa Barbara County Ranchos, (San Diego Historical Society)

King, T. H., *Report of Development of Ramona Irrigation District, November 3, 1925*, (Ramona Municipal Water District Records)

Kroeber, A. L., *Handbook of the Indians of California*, (Washington, D.C., U.S. Government Printing Office,1925)

Kunz, George F., *The Gem Mining of California, Bulletin # 37, (Sacramento, California State Mining Bureau, 1905)*

League of Women Voters of San Diego, *American Indians of San Diego County Census, 1974*, (San Diego Historical Society Collection)

LeMenager, Charles R., *Off the Main Road, a History of San Vicente and Barona*, (Ramona, Calif.,Eagle Peak Publishing Co., 1983)

Meyer, Ruth S., editor with Bowen, Russell and Ransom, Leona B., *Historic Buildings of the Ramona Area*, (Ramona, Calif., Ramona Pioneer Historical Society, 1975)

McKinstry, Dr. George, Jr., *Diaries, 1859-79*, (San Diego Historical Society Collection #221)

Mooney-LeVine And Associates, *Environmental Impact Statement Pamo Dam and Reservoir Project*, (U.S. Army Corps of Engineers, Los Angeles, Calif., October, 1986)

Moore, B.B., *Roads and Trails, 1769-1885 Map*, (County of San Diego, County Public Works Department, 1955)

Moore, Frances Atkinson, *Letter dated January 14, 1978*, (Ramona Pioneer Historical Society Collection)

Moriarty, Dr. James R. and Pierson, Larry J., *An Archaeological / Historical_Survey of the Ouderkirk Subdivision*, (San Diego, April 1979)

Northrup, Marie E., *Spanish - Mexican Families of Early California, 1769-1850*, (New Orleans, Polyaulhos, 1976)

Ogden, Adel, *Captain Henry Fitch, San Diego Merchant, 1825-1849*, (San Diego Historical Society, Journal of History, Fall 1981)

Ogden, Adel, *The California Sea Otter Trade, 1784-1848*, (Berkeley, University of California Press, 1941.)

Ogden, Adel, *Trading Vessels on the California Coast, 1786-1846*, (Typescript, San Diego Historical Society Collection)

Ortega, Francisco, *Letters, with Introduction by Thomas Workman Temple II*, (Historical Society of Southern California, Annual Publication, 1933)

Ortega, Jose Joaquin, *Letters to Pablo de la Gara 1863*, (Santa Barbara Mission Archives)

Pourade, Richard F., *The Silver Dons*, (San Diego, Union-Tribune Publishing Company, 1963)

Pourade, Richard F., *Gold in the Sun*, (San Diego, Union-Tribune Publishing Co., 1965)

Pourade, Richard F., *The Raising Tide*, (San Diego, Union-Tribune Publishing Company, 1967)

Pourade, Richard F., *City of the Dream*, (San Diego, Copley Books, 1977)

Peirce, Rollin, *Little Red Schoolhouse Days in Ramona*, (San Diego Historical Society Quarterly Journal, July 1960)

Peirce, Rollin W., *Story History of Ramona*, (Ramona, Typescript reprinted by Ramona Coordinating Council, August 1971)

Pitt, Leonard, *The Decline of the Californios*, (Berkeley, University of California Press, 1968)

Quincey, Martha Olivia (nee Billingsley), *Billingsley History in San Diego County, 1871 - 1945*, (Typescript, Ramona Pioneer Historical Society Collection, 1945)

Ramona High School, *History of Ramona Union Elementary School District*, (Ramona, Yearbook, El Ano, 1947)

Ramona Pioneer Historical Society, *Verlaque House*, (Typescript, RPHS Collection)

Ramona Sentinel, *Centennial Edition*, Three Sections, March 20, 1986

Rensch, Hero E., *Cullamac, Alias El Capitan Grande*, (San Diego Historical Society Quarterly, Vol. 11, No.3, 1956)

Robinson, W. W., *Land in California*, (Berkeley, University of California Press, 1948)

Roth, Linda, *The Ramona Castle: Irene Amy Strong's Home and the Craftsman Movement*, (San Diego Historical Society, Journal of History, Summer 1982)

Rush, Phillip S., *The Jack-Ass Mail*, (The Southern California Rancher, August 1957)

Rynerson, Fred, *Gems and Gold*, (Happy Camp, Calif.,Naturegraph Publishers, Inc., 1967)

San Diego Fitzgerald Volunteers, *Proceedings of the Court Martial of Antonio Garra, Jan 10-17,1852*, (Huntington Library Collection, San Marino, California)

San Diego County, Clerk of the Board Supervisors Office, Board Minutes.

San Diego County Recorder's Records; Deeds, Preemeption Claims, Homestead Grants, Recorder's Office

San Diego County, Assessment Records, 1850-1876; County Court Case Files, Civil and Criminal, 1850 - 1880; County Superintendent of Schools Records, School District Records, 1854-1920, San Diego Historical Society Collection

San Diego County, Official County Map, May 1872, M.G. Wheeler, County Engineer, County Public Works Department

San Diego County Water Authority, Annual Reports, 1946-1988, San Diego Historical Society Collection

Shinn, Charles Howard, *Pioneer Spanish Families of California*, (The Century Magazine, Jan. 1891, reprinted in the San Diego Historical Society Journal of History, June 1965)

Sinkankas, John, *Gemstones of North America*, (Princeton, N.J., D. Van Nostrand Company, Inc., 1959)

Sinkankas, John, *Largest American Gem Find in 42 Years*, (The Lapidary Journal, August, 1958)

Schwartz, John F., *San Diego County Treasurer's Correspondence*, (San Diego Historical Society Collection)

Stockton, Louis E., Interview by Edgar F. Hastings, Ramona, March 13, 1958, (Ramona Pioneer Historical Society Collection)

United States Land Commission Hearings, and U.S.District Court Proceedings, Southern California Division, Land Cases #191-SD and #195-SD, (Bancroft Library Collection, University of California, Berkeley)

United States Census, San Diego County 1850, 1860 and 1870, Ballena Township 1880, Santa Maria Township 1900 and Ramona Township 1910. (San Diego Historical Society Collection)

United States Geological Survey Maps, 1898, 1901 and 1902, (San Diego Historical Society Collection)

van Dam, Mary Augusta, *As I Remember Poway*, (Poway, Calif., Poway Historical Society, 2nd edition 1985)

Woodward, Arthur, *Out of the Past*, (Typescript, Ramona Pioneer Historical Society Collection)

Woodward, Arthur, *Notes on Showalter and Camp Wright*, (Ramona Pioneer Historical Society Collection)

Woodward, Arthur, *Indian Houses of Southern California*, (Los Angeles County Museum, leaflet series, 1949)

Woodward, Guy, *Early Day Postal History*, (Typescript, Ramona Pioneer Historical Society Collection)

Woodward, Guy, *Ramona and the Back Country*, (Typescript, Ramona Pioneer Historical Society Collection)

Acknowledgements

The author especially thanks those who graciously took time from their busy schedule to share their experiences and provide important information for this book.

Milt Angel, Jacque Beck, Dick Bottomley, Margo Brown, Gary Butterfield, Jane Cowgill, Lucy Cumming, Karl Diekman, Loretta Donham, Judy Endeman, Paul Engstrand, John Fansher, Dave Galusha, Fred Grand, Tom Griffin, Warren Henry, Jose Hurtado, Peggy Higley, Ethel Johnson, Barbara Kelly, Cynthia and Frank Kunkel, William Larson, Jim Laughlin, Paul Lewis, Mac McMacken, 'Old' Jim McWhorter, Jim Moriarty, Viola Peirce Miles, Dennis O'Leary, Al Pentis, Gertrude Page, Mary Kay Pinkard, Maureen Robertson, Rick Robertson, David Ross, Margaret Bargar Sander, M.J. 'Shelly' Shelton, Charles Snow, Fern Southcott, Lou Spaulding, Duane Spencer, Harold Stephen, Lois Stevens, Ann Sticka, Ray Stock, Larry Stirling, Betty Ann Tullock, Herb Walters, Glen Ward, Howard Welty, Don Wilson, Kenneth Woodward, Bob Wright, Donna and Gordon Zick --
--- and the person who spent the most time of all and was never too busy to help,
--- Guy Woodward

The author would like to give special thanks to Laura Brien for taking time from her busy schedule to help in the editorial and typesetting department, as well as to Paul Griffin who filled in at a difficult time to help us meet our production commitment.

Photos & Illustrations

A wide variety of photos is vital for a book of this kind. We want to again give our thanks to Guy for use of many photos from the Society's collection.

The staff at the San Diego Historical Society has always been very accommodating. Their great photo collection of San Diego heritage is unsurpassed. We wish to especially thank Jane and Larry Booth who run that operation and are always personally helpful and Tom Ademo who went out of his way for us on this project.

The author is most fortunate to have two great bothers in law who happen also to be talented illustrators. Thanks again to Ernie Prinzhorn of Pasadena who did the cover, and Jac Coté of Las Vegas, N.M. who illustrated the "Firing of the Anvil".

Louise Shidner is a descendant of one of Ramona's earliest pioneer families, the McIntoshs. Her great paintings of Ramona's early landmarks are currently displayed in the Ramona branch of the Bank of America. We wish to give our special thanks for permission to photograph some of those paintings for this book.

Photo Credits

Ramona Pioneer Historical Society, pages 44 top and bottom, 100, 103, 131, 143, 155, 157, 162, 163, 167, 174, and 213; San Diego Historical Society - Ticor Collection, pages 21, 36, 69, 76 top, 84, 87, 88, 97, 103, 104, 106, 129, 132, 133, 134, 136, 168 and 206; San Diego Historical Society - E.H. Davis Collection, page 20 top and bottom; Mary Ann Pentis, pages 189, 221 top and bottom; Margaret Barger Sander Collection, pages 70, 76 ,137 and 195; Bancroft Library, University of California, page 41 top and bottom; Rollin Peirce Collection, page 79 top and bottom; Louise Shidner paintings, pages 68, 104 and 163; Mary Kay Pinkard Collection, pages 208 and 209; James R. Moriarty Collection, pages 17 and 18; Harold Stephen Collection, 89 bottom; Gertrude Page Collection, page 81; Etcheverry Family Collection, page 85; Barbara Kelly Collection, page 155 bottom; Lucy Cumming Collection, page 207; Kunkel Collection, page 203; Automobile Club of Southern California, page 32; Ramona Fire Department, page 197; Ramona Municipal Water District, page 182; Forrest Letzring, page 188 top; Richard Bottomley Collection, page 169; Jac Cote cartoon, page 123. The balance of the photos and illustrations are by the author.

Index

About the Author

Charles LeMenager is by profession a land use and planning consultant. In recent years, however, he's spent more time at his avocations of researching and writing non-fiction, photography and piloting his Cessna Cardinal airplane.

He is a former corporate officer with the Fluor Corporation. Local and state government has also occupied much his time over the past thirty years, although mainly as a sideline. He is a former mayor and councilman in the City of Santa Rosa, California, a California State Director of Housing and Community Development under Governor Ronald Reagan and member of the Ramona Municipal Water District board.

He came to Ramona in 1970 to help master plan and develop the new community of San Diego Country Estates in the San Vicente Valley. He and wife Nancy liked the area so well they've made it their home ever since.

Other books by Mr. LeMenager include:

OFF THE MAIN ROAD
A History of the Rancho Cañada de San Vicente y Mesa del Padre Barona
1983, Second Edition 1990, ISBN 0-9611102-3-6
Eagle Peak Publishing Company, Ramona, California 92065

JULIAN CITY AND CUYAMACA COUNTRY
A History and Guide to the Past and Present
1992, ISBN 0-9611102-5-2 Hardcover
ISBN 0-9611102-4-4 Perfect Bound
Eagle Peak Publishing Company, Ramona, California 92065

FLYING AFTER 50
You're Not Too Old To Start
1995, ISBN 0-8138-2881-3
Iowa State University Press, Ames, Iowa 50014